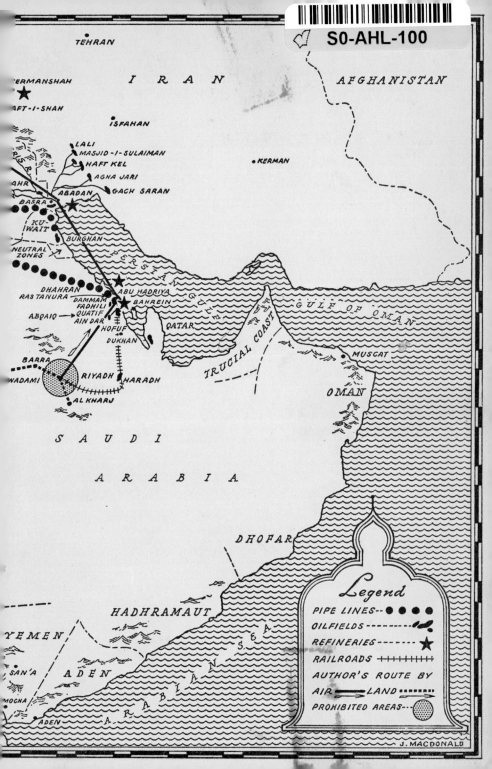

TEHRAN

I R A N

AFGHANISTAN

ERMANSHAH

AFT-I-SHAH

ISFAHAN

• KERMAN

LALI
MASJID-I-SULAIMAN
HAFT KEL
AGHA JARI
GACH SARAN

AHR

ABADAN

BASRA

KU-
WAIT

BURGHAN

NEUTRAL
ZONES

PERSIAN GULF

GULF OF OMAN

DHAHRAN
RAS TANURA

ABU HADRIYA

DAMMAM
FADHILI
QUATIF
AIN DAR

BAHREIN

ABQAIQ

HOFUF

QATAR

DUKHAN

TRUCIAL COAST

MUSCAT

BARRA

WADAMI

RIYADH

HARADH

AL KHARJ

OMAN

S A U D I

A R A B I A

DHOFAR

HADHRAMAUT

A R A B I A N *S E A*

YEMEN

SAN'A

ADEN

MOCHA

ADEN

Legend

PIPE LINES ●●●●

OILFIELDS

REFINERIES ★

RAILROADS ++++++

AUTHOR'S ROUTE BY

AIR ⟶ LAND ▪▪▪▪▪▪

PROHIBITED AREAS ⬤

J. MACDONALD

Tents and Towers of Arabia

"The strongest motive throughout had been a personal one, not mentioned here, but present to me, I think, every hour of these two years. Active pains and joys might fling up, like towers among my days: but, refluent as air, this hidden urge re-formed, to be the persisting element of life, till near the end."

T. E. LAWRENCE

Tents and Towers of Arabia

BY ROBERT SHAFFER

Illustrated with Photographs

DODD, MEAD & COMPANY · NEW YORK

TO
F. R. F.

Introduction

THE city of Jidda clings to the coral edge of the Tihama plain of the Hijaz province of Saudi Arabia. It is the aged and exhausted seaport for those mysterious and forbidden cities of Mecca and Medina; the gateway to the holy land of Islam. It exists because of the caprice of natural geography and historical events; caught between the warm waters and fiery *khamsins* of the Red Sea and febrile desolation of endless Arabian sand.

Jidda is dead with age and bleached white by constant exposure to the merciless, calcinating sun of hundreds and hundreds of years. It is hot and humid as only a city can be that has absorbed and preserved the moisture of the sea and the solar energy beamed upon it through ages of time. It pants feebly on the edge of the unwanted dross of creation, the seared wastes of Arabia which, ironically enough, float on lakes of black, liquid gold.

Introduction

To Jidda's heat, humidity and sandstorms has been added the plagues of the Pharaohs—locusts and flies; and because of its own antiquity and backwardness, the other modern annoyances of undependable plumbing and electricity, and always the eternal problem of WATER!

But it *is* the East; a fact which absolves its multitudes of faults, as only one can understand who has the East in his blood and is not aghast at its squalor, its poverty and filth, but instead loves its intoxicating odors, its customs and innate friendliness to all sympathetic natures.

To this spot I was sent, after having served amid the luxuries and pleasures of Egypt. The United States Department of State posted me there to represent our government and help administer the Anglo-American economic program that had been instituted for Saudi Arabia in pursuit of plans formulated for the prosecution of the war.

Frequent pains and rare pleasures were accentuated because of the austere setting, and became indeed, towers among our days, engraved upon our souls. I have attempted to record their existence, not with the full force of initial impressions, but in retrospect after time had softened the blows, permitting the virtues to remain the dominant memories.

Life in other Middle East countries had already imparted a degree of the Eastern attitude sufficient to enable my settling down to find that life, even in Arabia, could be a sentient experience, unexpectedly interesting and even enjoyable. This happy state was not reached without trials, however, and owed its accomplishment primarily to the fact that it was too hot to rebel for long, and in time one submitted and accepted; and therein lies the profound secret of Islam, the religious philosophy of that ancient land.

Contents

· *ix*

Contents

Illustrations

(Photographic supplement follows page 68)

His Majesty, Abdul Aziz Ibn Abdur-Rahman, with the Crown
    Prince

Street scene in Jeddah

Street scene in old Jeddah

King Ibn Saud with nineteen of his sons

The author with Donald

A typical Arab house in Jeddah

A captured viper on the desert in Saudi Arabia

Aerial view of an 'ain' at Al Kharj

View of Suq at capital city of Riyadh

The Great Mosque of Mecca—the congregation dispersing

Pilgrim tents crowd the plains between Medina and Mecca

*(The two photographs of Mecca are reproduced by courtesy of
Three Lions, Inc. All others by courtesy of Arabian American Oil
Co.)*

Endpaper maps drawn by James MacDonald

PART I

CHAPTER ONE

Gateway to the Holy Land of Islam

ALTHOUGH it was New Year's Eve when we left Cairo for the eight-hour flight down to Jidda, we hoped to celebrate the arrival of 1945 in Arabia. Egypt had experienced a terrific *shumal,* however, which flooded all the Nile Valley, and the continuing storm forced our plane down in Upper Egypt. The pilot put in at a tiny airport outside Luxor, the ancient Thebes, City of the Dead and Valley of Kings.

Luxor had received its "first rainfall in ninety-nine years," a stock remark whenever it does rain, and was a morass of black mud. The *fellaheen,* unaccustomed to rain and mud, plowed about in it like frightened insects caught on sticky flypaper, *galabiyas* clutched either waist high or thrown over their heads. Some wore baggy, white bloomers, but the younger ones, while covering their heads and faces, exposed only their full nakedness to the elements. Their labor and agitated expressions plainly indicated that such an act of Allah was a frightful experience indeed.

When the rain finally ceased we made a take-off from the black, water-soaked field and headed east toward the shores of the Red Sea, over swirls of mountains which looked like a devil's playground, and were again forced down by a *simoom* at Port Sudan in the Anglo-Egyptian Sudan.

The flying sand transformed day into night, and kept us grounded all day and into the night. This resulted in our spending a lonely New Year's Eve steaming in the Red Sea Hotel. The searing heat caused me to spend most of the time immersed in a tub of water, a highball beside me, while pondering what I had ever done to deserve such a fate and if I might ever extricate myself from it.

New Year's Day dawned clear and hot, however, and permitted an early take-off. We crossed the Red Sea and soon spotted the rolling wastes of Arabia. The plane followed the white ribbon of shoreline that modulated into the yellow and brown desolution of the Tihama plain, extending to the east until dissolving into nothing but mist. The sea came from the west, where it seemed joined with the sky in deep purple, fading to blue as it approached Arabia, then to emerald green where it touched the curving stretches of burning sand. Subterranean islands of coral, as well as a barrier reef, rose near to the surface, changing the water into spotted areas of the same brilliant green.

As the plane began to lose altitude, a distant village unbelievably appeared in the shimmering haze of heat. It assumed more distinct form as we rapidly approached, and it possessed the same bleached whiteness which endless time and constant sun produce on desert bones. It huddled close to the blue-green sea and held a wall about it as a protecting mantle from the desert furies of heat and sand. A few odd houses had strayed from its protection, as if wandering in delirium. One sprawling building, with its wooden skeleton showing, had boldly wandered as far as the airport where it appeared to have expired.

As the pilot came in for a landing it seemed we were dropping into an inferno that would envelop and consume us. The plane taxied to a stop and I thought we should all wither into moist dust before the door could be opened, but when we staggered out the desert heat struck even more fiercely. I could feel my face shrivel and my scalp creep as I gasped in astonishment, wondering that if this were winter, what would summer be like.

The plane was not expected, so the airport, a smoothed portion of desert, was vacant except for a Fordson lorry and its British driver. The plane quickly abandoned me as if seeking a kindlier land, and fled back across the sea to Africa and Eritrea.

The Englishman introduced himself as Willie, of the British Legation, and offered to take me to the house assigned by the Saudi Government to the Economic Mission. I knew the mission consisted of but one other American named Fred, and several Britishers, and that although Fred and I were Legation personnel, we would maintain a separate establishment. The Britishers were already there and Fred, too, had preceded me to get things started.

Willie drove along the rutted dusty road leading to the fortress-like Medina Gate, guarded by Arab police who saluted languorously as we passed through. Entering the city was like entering a hot bath, for the wall obstructed any breeze that might be fitfully stirring. The one main thoroughfare followed the wall, making its way around the entire city, turning now and then to avoid a house which seemed to have grown there unmindful of any plan or organization. In fact it was evident that the town had just grown as fancy led it, without plan or purpose, and where houses were clustered together, only enough space separated them to permit foot traffic; this lane or alley meandering as thoughtlessly as a woods path.

Inebriated buildings leaned slightly in unintended directions, staggering in the heat, and here and there helpfully supporting one another. Nevertheless they still maintained a sturdy and substantial appearance, rising four to six stories above the street; for the most part built of white coral blocks mortared with mud and interspersed occasionally with heavy gray beams. Their fronts were decorated from ground to roof with jutting upper stories, and huge latticed hanging balconies projected picturesquely into the streets. These latticed balconies were the *meshrabiya* of Egypt which in Arabia was called *shamiyah*. They were intricately hand-carved and weathered to whitish gray or brown. Tremendous doors opening onto inner courts were made of heavy teak-wood slabs, usually inset with a smaller door, all deeply carved and supported by huge wrought-iron hinges. In general the city gave the appearance of exaggerated Elizabethan architecture. The freedom of Arab imagination, however, had resulted in houses with elaborately fretted fronts, pierced and pargeted by an abundance of ornamental plasterwork.

A hushed, furtive atmosphere inhabited the town, making it seem as lifeless as the ancient Thebes so recently visited. No traffic nor people moved about, no green or living thing animated the scene. Only a few sleepy goats, unconcerned with our passing, were couched here and there in the shaded dust. The clean roadway and alleys had been packed down by animals and bare feet until solidified, and contained a top covering of fine damp dust, the thick nap of Jidda's natural carpet, which cushioned all sound.

I felt that Jidda had never been swept by a cleansing rain or a stiff breeze since the day it was built, but that it retained the same air, the same breath of multitudes from year to year, and would continue to as long as it should endure. It lacked all the vital qualities of other Eastern cities and instead had a sense of great age, lifelessness and exhaustion from long use, peculiar to itself alone.

As we passed a small lopsided mosque, its minaret leaning at a crazy angle, I remarked to Willie that the Tower of Pisa should feel quite at home if transplanted to Jidda. Willie laughingly agreed, then informed me that if one mentioned such matters to an Arab he would be reminded that only Allah is perfect. For an Arab to attempt such perfection as a true level or vertical line, either in building a house or in placing a tablecloth, would be considered as mocking God.

Willie deposited me at Beit Najib where I found our mission already well established; in fact the British members had been there for some time.

The British government, appreciating the value of Ibn Saud as a war ally, had assumed the major responsibility from 1941 onward for seeing that the impoverished country received sufficient foodstuffs, textiles, transport and other aid to meet its requirements. Prior to 1941 the Arabian American Oil Company had helped the king in his financial difficulties, although oil exports had only begun to be an important factor. Even though the war curtailed Aramco's activities, they continued to make advances against future royalties for they had already become an established member of the Saudi Arabian community. However, the country's economic isolation became so critical, as a result of the world shortages of goods and shipping and the continued absence of pilgrim traffic, as to be more than Aramco and the British government could cope with. The political and economic problems involved in Arabia's situation were not the responsibility of a private company, nor were they a matter for the consideration of the British alone; but not until 1944 did the United States feel sufficiently responsible or sympathetic to shoulder an equal share in the aid program.

Fred and I were sent to help administer the American side of the program and it was hoped that the maintenance of a minimum economy in Saudi Arabia would stabilize this critical area of the Arab world, a vital necessity in the winning of the war.

The first few weeks in Jidda were endured with many misgivings, for I was still untouched by the magic enchantment of legend and mystery associated with Arabia. For a Westerner to be suddenly dropped upon an alien land of cruel climate and primitive living, among seemingly unfriendly strangers, produced but a natural reaction, quite unappreciated at the time. The loneliness and desolation, though transient, became at times almost past bearing. Only gradually was there a revival of will to conquer the hostile climate and to win over a reticent people whose friendship was abundantly available only after the stranger had proved worthy.

Our daily lives quickly assumed a simple routine, arranged generally to best suit the individual's duties or inclinations, with the climate always a governing factor. I usually worked from daybreak until noon, avoiding the later office hours that provided the entire last half of the day for fishing or desert trips. Most sensible people attempted a siesta but to me little virtue was entailed in such effort. I preferred the freedom of sailing the sea or roaming the desert, although these diversions were usually a solitary experience. Our Christian Colony contained a total of fourteen Americans, but most of them preferred amusements of a more sedentary nature, or at least less strenuous ones. They were either more acclimated than I, or perhaps they had already learned the wisdom of offering little resistance to the indolent ways of the East.

CHAPTER TWO

The Boy Gazelle

Our house, Beit Najib, was one of the very few modern houses in Jidda. Being modern, it appeared as prominent as a boil and just about as lovely. It was a three-story stucco affair of jaundiced yellow and soiled white trim, the incredible result of the Arab builder's interpretation of modern architecture. The two upper floors had open terraced fronts, without the usual modesty of enclosing lattice-work. Its modern appearance seemed a discordant intrusion upon the mellow scene. Although its respectable neighbors appeared frowzy and tottering like senile old ladies tipsy with gin, they at least were veiled by delicate lattice and their eccentricities possessed the genteel dignity of age.

A third of our structure was devoted to broad central stairways and landings from which the various chambers opened on either side. The glazed tile floors were easily cleaned, but usually slippery wet with humidity. The ground floor was divided into storerooms, garage, lighting plant, pumproom and servants' quarters. The servants generously shared these quarters with a great assortment of insects, mice, stray goats and visiting friends. Kitchen and dining room occupied one side of the second floor and office space the other, while the third floor consisted of six bedrooms and a spacious living room.

Large, ineffectual fans, made in Eritrea, were set in the center of each high ceiling. The walls, rivuleted with moisture, were painted to simulate modernistic wallpaper, obtaining a most astonishing effect. The dining room was especially arresting and conveniently diverted one's attention from the food. It was probably intended for the harem, for a perverted artistic instinct had resulted in murals vaguely suggesting the Arab conception of the murals of Pompeii. Pieces of furniture were thoughtfully placed before the more frightening scenes, but we decided nothing should be done about the fertility motif upon the ceiling.

Beit Najib took its name from its Arab owner, as did all other Arab houses. There were no addresses in Jidda, every house being known by its name. Our own deformity was sparsely furnished, almost bare, with only large overstuffed chairs and sofas, mammoth wardrobes, unexpectedly modern dressing tables and mostiquaire-covered beds of a size sufficient for bundling with an entire harem. They were most uncomfortable, for the mattresses were supposed to be stuffed with corn husks, although I suspected when the manufacturer reached mine he had run short of husks and was obliged to use cobs instead. Their one fine feature, however, since we had no harem, was that ample room was provided for rolling and tossing from a sweated spot to a dry one during the sweltering nights.

We boasted a battery-set radio, so thoroughly pro-British that it refused to receive anything except BBC newscasts from London, with the demoralizing result that Fred and I often wondered if America was in the war at all.

Our lighting plant seemed as temperamental as any Russian. It was managed by a little black man whom we called *Nasir-Makaniki,* meaning Nasir-the-mechanic. Nasir was less than five feet tall and fearfully ugly. He was as comically ugly as a Negrillo Pygmy could be, for that is what he was. He came from one of the ancient and primitive Akka or Batwa tribes of equatorial Africa, and wore his hair frizzed to an immense halo in the manner of those people. A red tarbush perched atop it all.

This little man was very adept in his practice of black magic upon our engines and motors, but I recognized unused possibilities. Clothed in his natural expression, beneath the fezzed halo which only lacked a bone fillet for a final barbaric touch, in soiled shorts and tremendous overrun shoes, he could have been rented out as a means of frightening away evil spirits.

Through no fault of Nasir's, the lighting plant would co-operate with him only one day out of seven. Consequently, we were frequently obliged to use pressure lamps that raised the temperature another ten or twenty degrees. However, a little more did not matter materially since it was already too hot to live. The greatest inconvenience was the lack of refrigeration, for food would not keep from one meal to another and a cool drink was something unheard of. Air-conditioning was a luxury only the wealthy Beit Americani (Arabian American Oil Company) could afford or procure.

Lacking electricity, the pump, of course, would not pump, and water had to be carried up the stairs and poured into a tank on the roof, from where it ran by gravity to the *hammams* below. The sun heated it to a scalding temperature so that a cool shower was possible only early in the morning. As there were no sweet-water wells, the entire town depended on the *maya kadensa* which converted seawater into drinking water. When it broke down, as it often did, water was then transported from the holy Zemzem well in Mecca. All water was carried through the dusty streets to our house by water-carriers in open petrol tins, and was a priceless commodity despite its apparent impurity.

From the beginning the entire household suffered intermittently with dysentery and other undiagnosed ailments but seemed unconcerned with the cause. An attempt at forcing the servants to boil the drinking water proved futile. Then we made a soul-shaking discovery. When the pump happened to be in an operative mood, water was poured into a funnel that extended from the outside wall of the house. It flowed down to a sunken cement tank to be pumped from there to the one on the roof. This convenient funnel was being used by some of the street Arabs as a urinal!

At this point I undertook to clean the tank with the servants' limited help and moral support. We found it contained old shoes, broken crockery, a dead rat, a scum of drowned insects, several inches of muck and an old membership card to the Toledo Ohio Better Business Bureau! After a thorough cleaning and generous use of a strong purifier, most of our ills disappeared—probably because we ceased to drink water. The purifier lent the water a taste more horrible than its former impurities. On my own behalf I imported bottled mineral water from Eritrea. No one appreciated my efforts at the time but insisted I might have done this in the first place without spoiling that which they had to drink.

We were staffed with eight servants, all Somalis except two, but the house was run as if we had none. The cause for so many was that each servant in the East will perform only one specific task. Each considers himself a specialist, but this does not imply that he must be good at it. The cook will not wash dishes nor clean vegetables. Those jobs belong to a kitchen-boy. The *safragi* will not help one in with his luggage, for that is the job of the door-boy. And thus it goes.

Except for the Bedouin, Saudi Arabs did not perform manual, and certainly not domestic labor, all work being done by natives from the Anglo-Egyptian Sudan and Somaliland. They go to Jidda on the pilgrimage and remain in Arabia if their money runs out. Somalis probably make the best servants and can be very devoted and conscientious. They, like the Sudanese, are usually tall, strong and well built, with a mixture of Negro and Arab blood. Various tribal scars adorn their shiny black cheeks and foreheads, lending a dash of barbarism to their quiet, cool dignity.

Bukr was a good exponent of these characteristics except that he possessed an overdose of dignity. He was our door-boy, a seemingly necessary evil. Bukr usually maintained a rather surly, disagreeable sense of self-importance and was difficult to manage, one first having to convince him that any requested chore was within the scope of his duties. His *galabiya* was always spotless and his tarbush sported a tin replica of the British coat of arms. Bukr's vanity was traceable, we believed, to the fact that he once worked for the British Legation and always after nourished the notion that such a reference was the most superior of all requisites.

Bukr spent his few conscious moments studying ways and means to make us spend money. Of course he was far outrivaled by Ibrahim, whose urge followed a different bent and whose domestic difficulties alone provided fertile ground for excuses designed to lessen the weight of our cashbox. Bukr had a childish conception of the monetary system and innocently believed that all the money in the world belonged to the Americans and to the Minister of Finance, to whom even the king repaired when in need of cash.

It was necessary for me to open a personal account at the Dutch Bank and, for convenience, also at the British agents, Gellatly Hankey. When in need of additional *riyals* I simply sent a boy with a chit requesting the desired amount. This system, plus the fact that I converted dollars into Saudi riyals when their price was down, led to all manner of notions in the servants' minds concerning my financial status.

Bukr dreamed up the proposition one day that I should buy him a uniform; something in keeping with his distinguished position. He was proud of this position for it carried authority. As doorman he had the power to graciously permit entrance or firmly refuse it.

A little annoyed with Bukr, I thought the quickest end to the matter would be an open declaration of bankruptcy. In a tone of helplessness, I said, *"Mafeesh filoos!"* ("The money is finished, I haven't any.")

Bukr gazed at me with naïve innocence; then, as though solving a very simple financial problem for me, he dismissed the matter with a consoling, *"Maleesh!* (never mind)—just give me a chit to Gellatly Hankey. They still have plenty."

Bukr stood frowning before my desk one morning, dressed in his usual starched white *galabiya* that reached to the floor and looked like a long nightshirt. He finally announced in Arabic that a Bedou was at the door and that he had a baby gazelle for sale.

It seems that Bedouin follow gazelle herds in the desert until they find a newborn fawn too young to make its escape. Nature has provided the fawn with a protective camouflage coloring, since its young strength is not enough protection against the desert perils. At the approach of danger it flattens on the sand with an inborn sense of self-preservation, behind a hummock or salt bush where its mother has cunningly placed it. The herd dashes off and the mother returns later to seek her hidden fawn.

I have stood on the barren desert within ten yards of a young gazelle but could not spot it. Unfortunately they cannot always avoid the sharp eyes of the Bedou. The frightened creatures were often seen on the street, being pulled along by their captor toward the *suq* (market place) where they would be sold for meat or a household pet.

Since time immemorial the gazelle has played a part in the companionship of man. These charming creatures figured in man's life, art and poetry long before the dog became his devoted friend. It is recorded that thousands of years ago even Gotama, originator of Buddhism, found pleasure in a gazelle which befriended him when he was passing through the trials of his initiation. When Gotama awoke from a vision of horror he "took her in his arms, to warm her against his heart, and for a time sought refuge from the sorrows of the world in caressing a little gazelle."

With my ready permission, Bukr brought the barefoot, bearded man before me. In one ragged arm he carried a small silver-gray gazelle no larger than a kitten. Its long legs were as thin as a finger and its tiny hoofs were the size of a fingernail. It looked at me pathetically, with liquid brown eyes that seemed as melting as something inside me. I could only sit and stare, suddenly feeling excessively forlorn. In a moment I jumped up and carefully took the little thing into my arms where it snuggled comfortably. But for the staring black faces to check me, I think I would have yielded to the feeling to laugh or cry.

My face and actions no doubt betrayed me, for the shrewd Bedou hastily calculated a much higher price than the animal was worth. I tossed him what he asked, fearful he might even refuse me, and fled up the stairs to my room, the handful of silken softness held closely.

Bukr found a nipple somewhere in the *suq* as well as a baby's bottle, and Zaid obtained some fresh warm goat's milk. The gazelle nursed readily with unsuspected vigor, butting the bottle now and then and wagging his short black tail excitedly. When his sides became distended with milk, his nursing became less spirited until he slowed down and finally backed away. His eyes half closed in drowsiness while he licked the foam from his lips in contented speculation.

The gazelle was a diversion and I gladly neglected my work to feed and play with him. He dropped bouncing, small black pellets about the house as he scampered along in my footsteps, but Sayed, our young *safragi* was good-natured about it.

"*Maleesh!*" he declared. "*Al walad gazelle kwayis kitir!*" ("Never mind, the boy gazelle is very good.") He grinned fondly upon the animal while wielding a brush and dustpan.

Sayed was only a boy himself and still too young to have developed much character or physique. He cleaned with a will, made beds properly and mutely served table with rarely a *faux pas* more serious than first serving John, one of our robust British colleagues. A tolerance for his youthful efforts and a word of encouragement accomplished wonders with him. He was less trouble than all the other servants and Beit Najib would probably have ceased to function altogether had we ever lost him.

We could not continue calling the gazelle just "boy" but the name posed a problem. The servants all suggested Arab ones, but a gazelle named Mohammed or Abdullah sounded most absurd to me. Finally I stated he would be raised an American, with an American name, which appealed to them, and we finally settled on "Donald," which Fred also thought absurd. The servants were pleased, however, and I found their efforts at pronouncing the strange name most diverting.

Zaid, the Sudani messenger, was the most amusing, for every possible ounce of concentration seemed registered upon his shining, polished-black face. He first flexed his jaws then withdrew his lips, displaying a capacious red mouth full of beautiful white teeth. As he rolled his large black eyes heavenward until the whites shown, a strange sound slowly emerged which seemed to require great assistance on the part of his tongue. When his tongue finally got behind the sound, he looked at me expectantly, a little surprised with the result. I maintained a fairly straight face while advising that he could learn much easier by practicing before a mirror, but on handing him one, even he was overcome with laughter at such exaggerated facial contortions. The lesson always finished in an uproar.

CHAPTER THREE

Ibn Saud and Roosevelt

ABOUT this time, and for the first time in history, an American naval vessel called at an Arabian port. This fact was historic, but it was also the first occasion in twenty-two years for an American warship to pass completely through the Suez Canal.

Early one morning, just as the misty dawn lightened the eastern desert, the destroyer *U. S. S. Murphy* appeared beyond the barrier reef. By mere chance Mohammed Salamah, a Jidda pilot, happened to be waiting on the sea for the arrival of a Khedivial Line steamer expected that morning. With his aid the destroyer crept into the outer harbor and dropped anchor, to the surprise and consternation of all the Jidda citizenry except the very few who knew of its secret mission.

The ship's launch brought a number of the officers ashore and while the commander and the captain called on the American minister, the others strolled about to see that strange portal to the holy places of Islam. Being so completely foreign looking, but nevertheless unmistakably American, some street Arabs offered to show them where other Americans lived, and they were brought to Beit Najib. They were incredibly surprised to find two Americans living in such an out-of-the-way corner of the world, and even more so when they learned there were a total of fourteen in town.

The excitement and pleasure of unexpectedly seeing new faces, and American ones at that, rattled us so thoroughly that we ordered Sayed to bring quantities of cocktails, although it was only eleven in the morning. The early hour was no deterrent, however, for we often celebrated with much less cause.

That evening our minister, Colonel William A. Eddy, gave a reception for the ship's officers and invited all Christian residents and a number of prominent Arabs to meet them. We turned out about forty strong, and the moonlit roof of the legation resounded to much hilarity. The men seemed as happy to be on land as we were to have them. It was regretted that more of them could not have come ashore for at least a glimpse of the place, but perhaps their illusions of what Arabia should be were better served by their remaining on board.

After the party a few of the officers stopped at Beit Najib for a nightcap and to see the gazelle, about whom they had heard. Fred and I were then easily persuaded to return to the destroyer for a late supper. As the whaleboat threaded its careful way through the phosphorescent water, the stillness of the hour was broken by our boisterous rendition of the old navy favorite, "Roll Me Over," in a warm spirit of comradeship.

Aboard the destroyer we enjoyed a lavish feast of such American delicacies as rare roast beef, white bread, fresh butter and milk. The consumption of these ordinary things seemed like the food of gods to us after months of local fare. Whether or not Donald accompanied us to the ship is a vague question, but I feel confident if permitted any choice in the matter, he did not miss such an adventure.

By the next day everyone realized that the vessel had called on some vital mission, for the king, Ibn Saud, had arrived that same morning. His entry into Jidda, the first since conquering the Hijaz in 1926, was met with great excitement, although every precaution had been taken to keep the matter secret. Fear and speculation rapidly spread about the *suq,* the most amusing rumor being to the effect that His Majesty was being kidnapped by the American Government.

The captain gave an official luncheon that day aboard ship for the American Legation staff. Several officers had inquired the night before what foods we missed most and longed most to have. Without hesitation Fred and I had named our dreamed-of dishes, and had listed the most unprocurable our hungry minds could conceive. We drooled in anticipation as luncheon was served. It included thick juicy steaks, fresh vegetables, green salad and blueberry pie with ice cream.

After lunch we staggered on deck just as a large *dhow* loaded with countless fat-tailed sheep drew alongside. We, of course, immediately recognized the significance of this sight, but the navy personnel, knowing little about Arabia and its customs, were doubtless prepared for almost anything except the prospect of housing a herd of live sheep aboard the destroyer. The deck officer tried his best to send the dhow on its way but it was not easily dismissed. The Saudi official in charge insisted the sheep were to be loaded aboard the warship, for the king wished to supply the crew with fresh meat.

At this point Fred took a hand. He explained to the Saudi official, in Arabic, that the ship was well stocked and able to feed any number of people, and while the king's generosity was appreciated, there was little room on the destroyer for its necessary personnel, much less a herd of sheep. To avoid offending Arab hospitality, however, and since he knew the king and his party would be traveling on the vessel and would require fresh meat killed just before cooking and according to Moslem standards, he finally agreed that seven sheep should be swung aboard for the king's own use. These were transferred to the destroyer and stockaded on the fantail, over the stern, between two racks of depth charges. They were later slaughtered there, as required, and bled hanging from the rail.

Other dhows brought out quantities of rugs, gilded chairs, cooking utensils, immense copper trays for Arab-style eating and endless personal belongings of the king and his entourage.

A large tentlike canopy was pitched on the forward deck for the use of His Majesty, and the deck covered with rugs. A cabin had been arranged for him but he prefers, when at all possible, to be in the open and to sleep under canvas. He feels most at home under the stars. In consideration of his preferences, however, the pitching of "the big top" as the men termed the tent, lent a very odd appearance to a warship.

The royal party soon began to arrive and included several of the princes, various *sheikhs,* ministers, royal bodyguard and numerous servants such as the king's fortune teller, the official food taster, the royal purse bearer, the servers of ceremonial coffee, slaves, cooks and porters. There were forty-eight in all.

When the launch bearing His Majesty approached the destroyer, a loud blast echoed from the shore. It was a salute fired from the Saudi barracks outside the city wall. They had employed an ancient cannon which the Turks had left behind in 1916. This cannon was used only on state occasions and during the month of Ramadan. Its firing was always accompanied by much excitement for the report not only shook the city, but it was feared the gun would blow itself up someday, and the town along with it.

To the bosun's piping the royal launch drew alongside. All hands manned the rail and with full royal honors the ship began a twenty-one-gun salute. The first shot was a double one. It was later learned that the sailor firing the guns had stumbled in his excitement and tripped both guns at once. By some miracle they both fired simultaneously, doing no harm, but startling everyone by the extra loud blast.

As the king is arthritic and walks with difficulty, it was thought improbable that he would be able to navigate the ship's ladder. Plans had been made, therefore, to preclude such a necessity.

The sea had suddenly become quite rough and as the launch maneuvered beside the destroyer one of its sailors became drenched in the process. The launch was finally hoisted up and over the side, however, to where a platform had been erected for the king to step upon. While the guns blasted the air, the impassive-faced monarch prepared to descend from the launch to the deck as though the event were a common experience with him.

King Ibn Saud refused the arm of his brother, Emir Abdullah, and, turning to the young sailor who had been wet to the skin, took for assistance, his arm instead. Once on deck he turned to the boy, shook his hand and thanked him in a most friendly way.

The gesture made a great impression on all who witnessed it, but perhaps most of all on the young sailor himself. It was quite evident to all that despite position, Ibn Saud is still the simple desert chieftain. However, his simplicity does not imply poor manners, for he is most gracious and of tremendously impressive dignity.

The commander, the captain and our minister advanced to welcome the king. After these formalities they escorted him to the retirement of his tent forward. Anchor was raised and the *U. S. S. Murphy* headed north to its destination, a rendezvous with President Roosevelt in the Bitter Lakes of Egypt. This historic meeting marked the first occasion for Ibn Saud to leave his own country.

The king's retinue proceeded to set themselves up aboard ship in some rather startling fashions. The royal bakers prepared to bake bread in one of the handling rooms where powder and shot are passed into the gun turrets. They were finally persuaded to do their baking in the galley along with the royal cooks. Only the coffee-makers insisted on cooking over a charcoal brazier on deck. All food for the royal party was prepared by its own cooks but at every meal the king, who ate in his tent, was offered dishes from the ship's menu. He sampled and ate many of them and always accepted an American breakfast, served by one of the Negro mess boys.

During the first evening at sea the king was shown some newsreels and a color film entitled *Fighting Lady*. This was the story of an aircraft carrier and had been made up from official navy films, very skillfully and beautifully put together.

An interesting sidelight in regard to the king's viewing a film comes from the fact that all pictures, paintings, sculpture or anything which represents any living creature is forbidden by Islamic law as the "making of graven images." This explains why Arabic art consists of only geometric designs, flowers and arabesques. Some quick-thinking individual, however, explained to the king that moving pictures are only perfect records of objects, neither adding to nor detracting from them, whereas an artist impresses his own personality on his reproductions, thereby adding to the original and causing it to come under the tenets of the law. The king accepted this explanation with a twinkle in his eye and proceeded to enjoy the film.

In the middle of the first night at sea, after the king and his party had retired, a high wave broke over the bow, floating the rugs and nearly washing away the sleeping royalty. They quickly deserted their precarious shelter and for the rest of the trip His Majesty was content to sleep in the commander's stateroom, returning to his tent only to hold court in the daytime.

The ship's progress was met with strong head winds which caused it to roll and pitch as only destroyers can. The king remained undisturbed throughout the unusual experience but the rest of his party suffered acutely and spent much of the voyage in attitudes of prayer. For most of them it was their first time at sea. The king himself had only been on a ship once before, some twenty years past when he boarded a British sloop in the Persian Gulf to meet the King of Iraq. His inexperience did not affect him, however, and Colonel Eddy reported that on the occasion of their first dining together in the royal tent, the king took particular delight in making remarks which were designed to cause those whose stomachs were less certain to rush to the rail for relief.

By morning of the next day the sea had quieted somewhat and the sun burned hotly. His Majesty seated himself in his tent and each of the ship's officers was presented to him there. He was then given a demonstration of the ship's armament, to the amazement and childish delight of his party. The large guns and depth charges shook the ship from bow to stern, and although it must have been a startling revelation to the king, he alone remained serene and indifferent to the terrific jarring produced; not batting an eye, but simply nodding in thoughtful contemplation. While watching the antiaircraft fire, he used a pair of the ship's binoculars. Since he admired them, they were presented to him, along with several other things as mementos of his trip. His liking the binoculars provided a diplomatic opportunity, appreciated later, of making a present to him before he had a chance to give out any largess of his own.

In the evening the king entertained all the officers at dinner. The meal was served Arab-style on deck and was quite a treat to the men. Another short film was shown afterward of the naval battle off the Philippines, then the party retired for the night. By morning the destroyer had reached the Gulf of Suez, a long and surprisingly narrow body of water. A pilot was picked up at Suez and the ship entered the canal by nine o'clock.

The canal runs through two lakes, the Little and Great Bitter Lakes. The cruiser *U. S. S. Quincy,* carrying the President of the United States, was anchored in the larger and northernmost of these two bodies of water. She was sighted by ten o'clock and within an hour the *Murphy* drew alongside her.

The scene was an impressive one. All hands on both ships manned the rail in full honor of Ibn Saud. The canvas on the destroyer's deck had been removed and His Majesty sat in the only chair, facing the cruiser, with his brother, his sons, his ministers and counsellors standing behind him. When the ships had been secured together and a gangway placed across, he and his party, with Colonel Eddy, were piped over the side. Two of the king's personal bodyguards preceded him across the gangway. They were elaborately dressed in heavily gold-embroidered robes and jeweled daggers flashed at their sides; a marked contrast to the plain clothes worn by their sovereign. Those on the cruiser quite naturally supposed that two such resplendent creatures were at least of the royal blood and proceeded to give them full honors as intended for the king. The incident amused His Majesty as well as everyone else on the destroyer *Murphy.*

The royal party soon disappeared in the vastness of the cruiser where President Roosevelt awaited them. Thus the little-known but historic meeting took place between two of the most colorful figures of our time. The most rigorous secrecy was applied to the meeting, in pursuit of the policy which the press termed "the most petulant and malicious censorship in the world which was imposed on the recurring crises in the Middle East throughout the war." This secrecy was called "a cover for military blunders, Four Power rivalries and some of the fanciest double-dealing that even the cynical old Middle East had ever seen."

The ailing President was on his way home from the exacting demands of the Yalta Conference. Before leaving Yalta he had issued invitations for a personal interview to King Farouk of Egypt, Emperor Haile Selassie of Ethiopia and King Abdul Aziz of Saudi Arabia. It is reported that during the last evening in Yalta, the irascible Mr. Churchill was aghast to learn of the President's invitations to these three sovereigns, and that he viewed the matter with grave suspicion. He seemed to think there was some deep-laid plot afoot to undermine the British Empire in the Middle East. He was unable to learn the reason for these conferences without appealing to the President himself, and this he could not do. Instead, he announced the next morning that he too would go to Egypt, after a brief visit to Greece, for the purpose of seeing each of the sovereigns himself. He further stated that he had already sent messages asking them to remain in Egypt for conferences with him immediately after President Roosevelt left.

When Mr. Churchill learned of the further plan for transporting Ibn Saud as a guest of the American Navy, he lost no time in registering his irritation. Being well acquainted with British imperial jealousy, he no doubt considered it as contributing too much to American prestige and altogether too much an American "show" for British appetite in a quarter dubiously considered up to then as a sphere for their influence alone. With a pettiness unworthy of him he conveyed to President Roosevelt his suggestion that the king return to Arabia by means of a British warship. The President, it is said, assented with disarming generosity, but nevertheless to his intense amusement.

The interview on the *Quincy* between President Roosevelt and Ibn Saud was carried on through Colonel Eddy as interpreter and lasted over four hours. It involved the questions of the place of the Middle East in the war effort, the Palestine problem, organization of the United Nations and the oil resources of Saudi Arabia in which American interests hold concession.

The Arab states greatly feared the penetration of Russian influence into the Middle East, more than they had the German, but at the time of this meeting they were more immediately concerned with the possibility of a Jewish state in Palestine. In the interests of justice, as well as our own national advantage, we were formulating policy which favored the Arab states. Our strongest efforts had been directed toward winning Arab friendship and demonstrating our sympathetic understanding of their many difficulties. Outside interests have always added to the smouldering volcano of political agitation in the Middle East, but only a limited and prejudiced understanding of many complex factors could cause one to believe that American interests were purely selfish and due alone to the oil question involved, as has been claimed.

The discussion of the Palestine problem was very short and to the point. The President asked Ibn Saud if he would countenance any further limited immigration into Palestine and seemed surprised at the king's blunt refusal. Evidently he could not believe it, for he returned to the subject several times, until the king launched into an extended explanation setting forth the Arab position and their determination to resist further immigration to the point where they would rally to a *Jihad* (a Moslem holy war) and fight to the last man before permitting the formation of a Jewish state.

This was probably the first time President Roosevelt realized the extent of Arab determination and perhaps the point to which he referred when later he said that he had learned more about the situation in five minutes' conversation with Ibn Saud than he had learned in years of study.

The President finally gave the king unequivocal assurance of our continued and unfailing friendship and promised that no decision would be taken with respect to the basic situation in Palestine without first holding full consultation with both Arabs and Jews. His Majesty was grateful for this confidence and the President later reiterated his promise in a letter to the king, in his capacity as Chief of the Executive Branch of the United States Government, not to support any solution of the problem without prior clearance of the matter with the king, nor to take any action which might prove hostile to the Arab people.*

Before taking leave of President Roosevelt, Ibn Saud presented him with many rich presents. The President in turn offered to send a wheelchair such as his own for the king's use, since he had admired it so greatly.†

The king and his party returned to the destroyer *Murphy* and within a few moments the *Quincy* weighed anchor and departed for Alexandria to keep the President's appointments with King Farouk and Emperor Haile Selassie.

Back on the destroyer, Ibn Saud proceeded to hand out gifts to the

---

* After the death of President Roosevelt we seemed to adopt a perfidious attitude toward the Arabs, an attitude which they considered betrayal. In this connection the question arose regarding the commitments made to Saudi Arabia. The State Department denied that such commitments existed as the Saudis claimed, whereupon the Saudi government offered to produce the documents. The Department did not know of their existence but a search revealed them to be in the White House archives. The exchange of letters between President Roosevelt and Ibn Saud were then published in the *New York Times* of October 19, 1945.

† After its arrival in Riyadh the king always pointed it out proudly along with a signed photograph as "the gift from my friend, President Roosevelt" and exhibited more pleasure in the chair than in the gift which came later—a luxurious C-47 passenger plane.

entire personnel aboard. It is his custom on such occasions, but in this instance he felt deeply grateful for the way he and his party had been treated and for all the efforts made in the interest of their comfort and safety. Apparently only he, of all the party, fully realized the difficulty of accommodating half a hundred additional persons on a destroyer which under normal circumstances is always very crowded.

To the captain and commander the king presented complete Arab costumes and gold daggers; to the nineteen officers, Arab costumes and gold watches; to the thirteen petty officers, fifteen Egyptian pounds each (over $60); and to each of the 256 enlisted men, ten Egyptian pounds each (over $40). The gifts were a complete surprise to everyone and each felt singularly honored.

The destroyer remained anchored in the Great Bitter Lake overnight awaiting the arrival of the British Minister to Saudi Arabia. When he arrived next morning he presented Ibn Saud with the plans which had been made for him. These were accepted, and the destroyer then weighed anchor and headed for the port of Ismailia in Egypt. Port was reached by sundown and the royal party was immediately put ashore. A fleet of British motorcars stood waiting to speed them to the small oasis of Fayum outside Cairo for the meeting with Mr. Churchill.

The American minister and his party left the *Murphy* at Ismailia, the minister flying on to Alexandria to catch up with the *Quincy* for further conferences with the President and Secretary of State Edward R. Stettinius, Jr. The *Murphy* also left Ismailia at once to rejoin the President's waiting ship, whence it had come in the first place.

After his interview with Mr. Churchill, Ibn Saud proceeded into Cairo as guest of King Farouk. A parade was held in his honor through the crowded streets that had been covered with a layer of fine sand and had been decorated with bunting, flags and banners and high arches. Thousands of people lined the streets to see the spectacle of the two leading Moslem monarchs riding together in an open carriage drawn by six white Arab stallions. Those of us who were in Cairo watched the procession from a balcony at Shepheards Hotel. When Ibn Saud was later asked what had impressed him most on his trip, he replied that he was most startled, if not shocked, at the great number of unveiled women seen on the streets of Cairo.

While in Egypt, His Majesty attended a Pan-Arab conference of five other Arab States that was held at Abdine Palace in Cairo. The conference caused the Middle East to bubble and boil with the usual rumors, fears, hopes and suspicions. Saudi Arabia declared war on Germany and Japan, as did Egypt and Turkey, for President Roosevelt had requested that these declarations be made not later than a given date, thus establishing their eligibility to the United Nations.

While it is true that their neutrality alone had constituted an asset during the war, it is also true that until this time Egypt and Turkey had been content merely to absorb Allied economic assistance, and when requested to make their declarations were quite prepared to consider it the eleventh hour of their chances for cutting in on postwar advantages.

His Majesty, Ibn Saud, returned to Jidda and his joyous subjects aboard a war-marked British cruiser, *H. M. S. Aurora.* Jidda was gaily decorated for the occasion with flags and numerous triumphal arches. Tribes converged from all over Arabia to welcome their sovereign, causing the town to assume a carnival air. All the European colony gathered on the terrace of Beit Najib from where we could see the king step ashore and into his waiting automobile.

The American minister and his party had flown back by this time and Colonel Eddy was highly amused to learn of the various rumors that had been spread concerning the king's voyage, despite the severe censorship. In making his report to Washington, Colonel Eddy expressed this phase of the matter in his own inimitable style:

"The king's departure from Jidda caused an eruption of rumors in the market place, ever pregnant with litters of rumors delivered daily in the hope that one might survive."

The king's departure proved so eventful, the minister's remark might well have applied to the reaction it caused throughout the entire world.

CHAPTER FOUR

A Black Head Rolls in the Dust

Donald soon became housebroken, and the process was easy enough. He enjoyed the freedom of the entire house but seldom permitted me out of sight, following my movements from morning until night. He was content for awhile to sleep under my bed but when strong enough to leap upon it, preferred to sleep in bed with me rather than on the floor. While still so young, it was necessary to feed him every few hours, and appearance of the bottle made him joyously excited. He chased me to the feeding spot on the terrace, kicking up his heels and butting my legs until the bottle was lowered within reach. He nursed greedily until his sides looked dangerously inflated. When satisfied, he staggered stiffly a step or two and drowsily licked away the foamy mustache created in the process. At this point I placed him on a low sandbox where, by touching his sensitive little tail, he stooped to avoid the tickling. The stooped position immediately produced the idea, for he was ready to burst anyway. From then on he stepped into the box of his own volition.

Though at first lonely for something to expend our affections upon, the number of creatures we soon acquired rapidly increased to the proportions of a menagerie. In addition to Donald there were two Eritrean fowl, said to be turkeys, fattening on the roof; two white rabbits which John insisted on bringing to the living room at tea-time (because he was fattening them up also); a *pariah* puppy and two large wild gazelles also secluded on the roof. These I bought merely to thwart their captor, intending to give them their freedom far from town in familiar surroundings. The news of my sympathy for gazelles spread and any Bedou leading one was sent by all, including the gate policemen, direct to Beit Najib. The price of these animals went into an inflationary spiral, but I paid with the satisfaction of knowing that fewer reached the market to be abused and eaten. I felt more than repaid by the companionship of Donald and by his growing devotion.

About this time, I decided one night to sleep on the desert. The constant pain of enervating heat and humidity was one thing, but when it prevented sleep for weeks on end, madness seemed only around the corner. One seemed to drink then with a certain desperation, hoping that alcohol might at least induce sleep if not prevent insanity.

During the night when it seemed even my brain was melting away to join the sweat coursing down my body, I grabbed several blankets and fled down the stairs followed by Donald. We climbed into the jeep and headed for the foothills toward Mecca. When the air became cooler I pulled off the road, spread the blankets and dropped upon them, careless of any wolves, hyenas or anything else that might be about.

The great empty plain, bright with moonlight, swept down to the sea where nestled Jidda, white and silvered in the silent night. The city seemed to lie in a valley, for the sea beyond slowly inclined until it met with the sky.

Man's body might be tortured by the heat of day and the humidity of night in the walled city, but at least for his soul, Allah decreed that the Arabian nights should preserve their pristine peace and calm.

I gazed into the star-studded, dark-blue canopy overhead while Donald flitted whimsically about like a moonsprite, chasing and being chased by fantasies of his own playful conjuring. A whispering, warm breeze stirred about the desert but it was possible to breathe and to become dry. I quickly drifted into sleep, conscious of the gazelle settling down close beside me.

The far-off cry of a Jidda *muezzin* crept into my sleep. His call was an insistent, tantalizing thread of sound which reached out to gently coax me back to consciousness. The sun had not appeared but the desert was a desolate paradise of misty, white light and colorless sand, pleasantly tempered yet pregnant with the threat of wracking heat soon to follow.

Refreshed and lighthearted we rode back to enter the stagnant, moist warmth of Jidda, prepared to face another day.

Donald watched me shower and dress with little interest, as if it were an old story, an unnecessary delay. He finally trotted off toward the dining room and when I later descended he stood waiting at the door. It never mattered that everyone else might already be there. He would not enter but waited patiently for me as if it were part of his peculiar code of loyalty. After we entered he might accept a morsel if called to someone's side, but he preferred to stand close beside me where I could easily slip him the things he liked.

Only John was seated at the table this morning. John was the only civilian of our three British colleagues. He acted as billet secretary, handling all accounts both office and household, as well as ordering supplies and bossing the servants; all with unfortunately meager results. While only twenty-four years old, John had already attained the figure of an Egyptian *pasha* and was a sight to behold in khaki shorts.

John sat spread over the table, his straight black hair hanging carelessly over an already sweat-covered brow. Thick-lensed glasses accentuated his cunning eyes. Sayed at once brought on several platters of food and served me first, passing them to John who scooped all that remained onto his own plate. The boy had orders to always serve clockwise, thus permitting John to be served last. This was necessary since John always scraped the platters clean and unless served last, others might suffer from his thoughtlessness.

John proceeded to drench the mountain of food before him with oil, vinegar, salt, pepper, Worcestershire sauce and ketchup. The unappetizing sight was then thoroughly mixed by a fork held in one hand and a knife in the other, as a chef would mix a salad. John then pierced a collection onto the fork prongs and banked it far up the handle with the aid of his knife. The food was assembled and shoveled into his mouth by the left hand with a speed and efficiency which caused me to stare rudely in fascination.

John carried on an active, animated conversation meanwhile which did not permit any chewing. The food obligingly slid down his throat, however, as fast as thrown into the maw, totally unmindful of any mastication.

John was much excited for the news had become official that a public beheading would be held in the square beyond Beit Najib. He was pleased to be able to explain to me that according to Sharia

(Koranic) Law, the crimes punishable by death are treason, murder and dacoity; that is, robbery by one of a gang of murderous thieves. Adultery is also a crime in Arabia, punishable by death, for although desert Arabs are said to be bestial in sex, they are nevertheless extremely severe in dealing out punishment and are aghast at the unpunished adultery in other countries. It is well said that if a man of Arabia seeks lecheries he must go to the great cities of other countries.

In judging a crime, certain circumstances may lead to alleviation of the death punishment, so in this sense it is not mandatory. In cases of murder, for instance, where the murderer's intention is doubtful, blood money may be decreed. The punishment to be inflicted in any particular case thus depends upon the circumstances involved.

In this instance a Takruni had been duly convicted of murder under Sharia Law, as administered by the local authorities. The king had confirmed their decision and had pronounced sentence.

The execution was scheduled for three o'clock, but early in the day the square began to fill with many people and a bedlam of noise. Dervishes and sword dancers entertained the dense crowds, infecting them with their own fevered excitement. As the hour approached it seemed everyone in Jidda had assembled, from ragged Bedouin to richly dressed merchants. The entire European colony gathered on our terraces overlooking the spot where the act would take place. We seemed silently to dread the prospect of the tragedy soon to be enacted, unable to converse or to act naturally.

A number of officials finally made their way through the throng, held back by Saudi police, and mounted the small platform raised for the occasion. At their appearance the multitude became motionless and silent, and the scene assumed unreality, for not even the footsteps produced any sound.

A dozen Saudi soldiers followed, but no sounds paced them forward either. Two in the center held the condemned man between them, aiding him forward. The hands of the wretch were tied behind him and his black face appeared paralyzed with fear. Only a sarong covered his lean nakedness. The official executioner brought up the rear along with his sword bearer.

The formalities of the execution were performed in cold justice, deliberately and with dignity. An official read off the charge and the consequent sentence. Without further ceremony the man was pushed forward, unresisting. He was forced to his knees and his head bent forward. He remained there immobile, as a *mullah* began to read from the Koran.

The executioner quickly stepped forward. He was a black giant from the Najd, said to be the king's slave. Rolling up the sleeves of his gown in a purposeful manner, he reached for one of the swords. Four feet of thin Damascus steel glinted in the sunlight as the blade was slowly withdrawn from its scabbard. He hefted it once in an efficient weighing gesture. The silence was oppressive. I expected some hysterical sound, a scream perhaps, which would release the violence gathered and smouldering below.

Without ado the headsman pricked the Takruni's neck with the sword point. It produced the desired involuntary reaction of tight, solid muscles. As quickly, the blade was raised high, grasped in both hands. It cut the air with a clean sound in its downward stroke. The bare, black head dropped neatly from the body almost too quickly for the eye to see. I scarcely caught its quick severing, but I did see it roll in the dust before the body slowly fell forward upon it. A terrific gush of brilliant red followed in a second from the ugly stump. It spurted several feet in a red arc with each diminishing heart throb, as the body shuttered and jerked, now unwilling and resisting.

As the red life flowed forth to make an ugly dark puddle upon the unabsorbing gray dust, a sound arose from the crowd. It seemed like a tremendous exhalation, a bursting sound of released breath and passion. Then voices were heard, rising slowly to a deafening crescendo.

We turned into the house quickly, each white and faint and carrying a horror not of this day.

CHAPTER FIVE

Two-Riyal Ibrahim

OLD HAMID pretended to be the cook, but it developed as I suspected from the first meal, that he had been only a dish-wash boy before coming to us. Hamid was of an indeterminate age and wore as loose and tired an expression as his old straw slippers. In skull-cap and soiled *galabiya,* he patiently listened to my admonitions about dirt while nodding affirmatively and murmuring, *"Iwa, iwa"* (yes, yes) and then persistently doing as he pleased. He thought cleanliness of any kind strictly an American eccentricity, for dirt was a natural thing and never hurt anyone—*insha' Allah!* (God willing), of course. His culinary ideas, or rather lack of them, would have filled volumes and his only reliable dish was lamb curry, which we had with exasperating frequency. I am certain Hamid would not have hesitated to serve it for breakfast if the disagreeable dish would only have kept from the preceding meal.

Hamid required a pint of oil with which to fry canned bacon, and then merely dragged the bacon through the oil and served it barely warmed. His idea of fried eggs was to serve them raw looking and quivering in a puddle of grease. All efforts to improve such conceptions were met with a careless, *"maleesh!"*—it doesn't matter, to express its unimportance.

Although I occasionally teased him, I felt sorry for old Hamid and determined to charitably endure his cooking until my health should become impaired. At that point I intended to take a hand, insist that he be let go with a good gift and our blessing and then train Fadl for the job.

Fadl was the dish-wash boy, black as ebony and handsomely decorated on each cheek with a long and fancy Sudanese tribal scar. I had noticed that he was anxious to learn to cook, and he seemed young and pliable enough to absorb some instruction. I communicated my future hopes to him in confidence and found him intrigued to learn that American men can cook. He stood before me in confused shyness, hanging his head and only occasionally permitting a quick glance of sparkling dark eyes.

"Iwa, iwa," he promised, "I will make a good cook, *insha' Allah."*

Fadl was willing and I liked him, but Allah, I felt sure, would have little to do with teaching him to cook. That responsibility would be mine.

Of all the servants, only one actually caused any serious headaches, but then, he also provided the most amusement. This was Ibrahim, of undefined position, and a most unnecessary thorn in our overheated flesh.

Ibrahim could easily have qualified for the unfilled position of town idiot. He wore an ear-to-ear grin as faithfully as he wore pants. His assorted wardrobe had been collected from a dozen different nations, all of whom he had worked for, and some of the combinations were so striking as to tax one's credulity. It was not unusual for him to wear three hats at one time: a *kufi,* a tarbush, and these topped by an American Air Force cap that I had given him.

Ibrahim was of average height and composed of only skin and bones and large white teeth. There was no normal shape to his body and there were strings where muscles should have been. His black skinny legs were widely bowed and had the same circumference at any point— ankle, calf or thigh. His feet were the only substantial things about him and they were always bare, since he had never found a pair of shoes to fit them.

Ibrahim's duties, if any at all, consisted of anything he could be wheedled into, either by command, persuasion, promise of reward or threats of beheading. He was well aware that heads still rolled oc- casionally at the king's pleasure, so when completely exasperated, I reminded him that if the king only knew of his worthlessness he would surely give the order for his beheading.

The rascal probably held some trump card of protection of which I was ignorant, for he only grinned at the picture I drew of his demise and regarded my threats with amused skepticism expressed in much tongue-clicking and many denying *"la, la's."* When I arrived at the feeling that any more traffic with Ibrahim would surely induce a nervous breakdown, I watched for a similar mood in Fred, then demanded to know why we retained Ibrahim and went to such ex- tremes of paying someone to drive us mad when abundant natural forces were provided.

"What good is he," I reasoned, "except to add to our already in- numerable difficulties?"

Fred agreed, but when pressed for a decision, half-heartedly admitted that the only redeeming feature of Ibrahim's existence was a certain "entertainment value." Here I had to concede, for Ibrahim was always good for a laugh, if for no other reason than his appearance, although I questioned such worth when weighed against his pestering habits.

In fairness even to Ibrahim, it must be admitted that he did justify himself somewhat after we acquired the gazelle. He was the first to be able to pronounce Donald's name so that it was at all recognizable either to me or the animal. He became Donald's devoted guard and often brought him *berseem* (clover) which he would not eat but did enjoy scattering about the house.

Ibrahim always loitered about the door except when he might be wanted, then could never be found. He made an appearance every night as if expecting to spend a pleasant and sociable evening, and if anyone had ever been rash enough to say, "have a chair Ibrahim," I am positive he would have taken it without batting an eye. However, he merely stood at the door in his conception of soldierly dignity, wide British shorts failing to hide the great arc of his skinny, bowed legs. The fixed grin on his black face was only stopped by his ears. The Air Force cap shaded his dancing eyes.

Fred and I continued talking, determined to ignore him to the limit of our endurance. Ibrahim continued to maintain his fixed posture, grin and all, for as long as necessary before Fred broke down.

"Well, Ibrahim," he laughed, "what do you want?"

It was the fatal opening, for out it came with unashamed simplicity. Ibrahim needed two riyals, as always; never more, never less. It might be for anything from feed for the turkeys on the roof to a down payment on a new wife. He never left until the money was handed over, and we were always glad to do this in the end. It was the only way to get rid of him.

We gave a party at this time for some visiting army officers and their staff. In the course of the evening I was astounded to see Ibrahim circulating among the guests. Although his help had not been solicited, he was passing *canapés* about the room. A clean *galabiya* had been tactfully pulled over his other clothes, but for the occasion he had retained the Air Force cap—and at a jaunty angle too. I reached him in time to intercept his approach to General Wilson, and grabbing the plate demanded *sotto voce,*

"Ibrahim! what the devil are you doing here?"

"Serving our guests," he blithely replied in Arabic, as if I had posed a foolish question.

I sternly demanded he take himself to any far-removed place, so long as it was out of my sight.

Next morning Ibrahim appeared at the doorway as we breakfasted. Fred looked up to ask,

"Well, Ibrahim, how did you enjoy the party?"

Ibrahim's reply was so casual I could have kicked him. In Arabic intelligible enough for anyone to understand, he said, "Oh, I had a wonderful time. . . . I think we entertain as well as anyone in Jidda!"

Ibrahim had made himself part of our household, and I knew he was there to stay.

CHAPTER SIX

What, No Women?

JIDDA was a city without women. Factually this was untrue, but as a practical matter the statement is quite correct. There were only seven white women altogether in our small colony. They were the wives of various government officials and of several foreign business men. Though limited in number, they represented a good assortment of nationalities; American, British, French, Dutch and Egyptian, with a motherly White Russian refugee added for good measure. Even this small number often decreased to none whatever when they were all away in Egypt or their homelands at the same time. When that happened the small cocktail and dinner parties were dreary affairs indeed. But it was necessary for them to get away since women cannot endure the climate of Arabia as well as men. They needed a change every few months either by going to the beaches of Alexandria or to the cool air of the Lebanese mountains. It was a fortunate man, however, who could escape even once in six months for a breath of cooler air or a sample of the flesh-pots of Egypt. Men were expected to be built of sterner stuff.

When we were lucky enough to have several of these wives in our midst, they always proved to be most gracious and sociable. Despite the climate or any locally-induced ills, they always turned out for the parties as a matter of Christian duty. Their reward was the undivided attention of the entire lot of lonely men, and although the evening may have been too sweltering for man or beast, they were sporting enough to dance until ready to drop.

These ladies, it must be added, were not usually young and attractive enough to cause serious complications, even though the least attractive appeared most seductive after one had been resident awhile. Their dressing each evening for dinner seemed pathetically brave, but was doubtless essential to their own morale, and contributed to ours as well.

Whenever an American plane stopped at Jidda the GI crews always asked, immediately they set foot on the ground, "Where are the women?" "What women?" we always retorted. "Haven't you ever heard about Arabia?"

They all seemed to possess the illusion that Arabia is synonymous with beautiful women, and felt quite defrauded when informed that any women in the land were safely hidden behind closed doors and latticed windows.

"What do you *do* for women?" they asked next, in a practical American manner.

"What do *you* do," we returned, "when you haven't something? You do without, don't you?"

They shook their heads thoughtfully over this, as if such philosophy had never occurred to them. Fred had any number of shocking retorts with which to vary the reply when we grew weary of the regular routine. Some of them were so startling as to produce the desired result—the tired subject was changed to something else immediately. One incredulous young fellow was thoroughly shocked when someone replied to the usual question with the Rabelaisian rejoinder, *"Women? Nonsense! We have plenty of goats!"*

The life was difficult for men, worse for women and sheer tragedy for any white woman married to a Moslem. It meant that they must observe all Moslem customs and enter *purdah,* which not only entailed veiling but strict seclusion in the harem.

There remains a general misconception about a harem in Western minds. In the first place it is pronounced *"hareem"* and secondly, it does not necessarily mean a bevy of beauties as depicted in *Esquire*. It does mean the wives and other females of a household when mentioned collectively, but it also denotes the particular quarters allotted to them.

A more important matter, however, is the common mistake so often made in using the expression "Mohammedan" or "Mohammedanism." To quote the authority, R. V. C. Bodley: "These words were never used by Mohammed and his disciples. In spite of the reverence for their Prophet, these designations have always been rejected by the Faithful. 'Moslem, one who surrenders himself to the Will of God,' is the only correct term to apply to a member of the religion which Mohammed founded."

One of the king's ministers was a Palestinian Arab. Although not a Saudi national he was nevertheless subject while in Arabia to Saudi rule. He was a Moslem, of course, but married to a very beautiful and cultured Parisienne, a much-traveled woman of broad interests and learning. She usually resided in Egypt while awaiting the expiration of her husband's appointment, but was persuaded by him to spend several months in Jidda on a visit.

Madame arrived in due course, along with their only child, a little girl. As a welcoming gesture the king sent a present for the child— a little slave girl of the same age. The children played together happily, each realizing, however, their strange relation to each other. As a rule there existed a touching companionship between them as they played like any other children. But in childish tantrums the little French girl was not above asserting the paradox of complete ownership over her playmate. She sometimes threatened to have her beaten if she did not obey, or else sold or returned to the palace. On these occasions the little dark face clouded and tears hung in her black eyes. Otherwise she accepted her role with a patience which reminded me of the docile, uncomplaining donkeys seen in the *suq*.

The minister and his wife were obliged to abide by all Moslem and Saudi customs, despite their advanced or Westernized ideas. As madame naturally desired the intellectual society of her own kind, it was necessary to confine all association with mixed non-Moslems to small gatherings held late in the evening and in the strictest secrecy after all servants had been dismissed from the house. She could, of course, entertain any women friends whenever she wished, but the mixed parties were rather furtive affairs.

As the restricted existence began to pall, madame was finally persuaded by Mrs. Eddy, the American minister's wife, to attend one of the weekly film showings. These were held on the roof terrace of the minister's residence located far beyond the city walls, and were open to all the European colony. Mrs. Eddy suggested that if madame arrived heavily veiled, in the dark and after the picture began, she would never be noticed.

She did attend one night, accompanied by her husband, arriving late and leaving before the lights were again turned up. It was felt that she at least had one evening of limited freedom and entertainment. The following day her husband was summoned to the palace at Riyadh. He made the long trip and when received by the king was severely reprimanded. In some way the occurrence had leaked out and its news reached the king with the speed of the telephone. As a penalty His Majesty pronounced that the lady in question was never again to leave the confines of her harem as long as she remained in Saudi Arabia, and she of course could never leave the country without his permission.

After that I always felt on passing their house, that I was passing a sixteenth-century jail, wherein the lovely lady languished. Many months later she succeeded in obtaining the king's permission to leave her prison and to depart from Arabia. The slave-child was not sold, but instead returned to the familiar surroundings of the king's household.

The king's sentence in this case was a stern one, but not indicative of any personal backwardness or narrowmindedness on his part. As the leading spiritual force of Islam, he is expected by the great mass of fanatical, ignorant and prejudiced followers to severely enforce such customs as strict confinement of all females and denial of the freedom of social intercourse in mixed gatherings of unbelievers. The pressure of an austere religion was a compelling reason for so severe a punishment.

Several American women had lived in Arab harems. At one time the king invited an American nurse to visit his palace in Riyadh. Several of his wives were ailing and required whatever medical attention could be secured. The American nurse was adventurous enough to accept the rare honor and until very recently she remained the only American woman ever to have entered Riyadh. She lived in the harem while there, in the same seclusion accorded the women of the royal household.

Her stories about the experience are not for me to recount, except possibly to mention the interest which the women took in her clothes. They examined her from skin out. When the old queen, who had become decidedly stout, learned the purpose of Ruby's girdle, her eyes assumed a covetous light. She begged the nurse for the girdle, but Ruby protested that the queen could not possibly get into it. However, she was obliged to agree that if the old lady could get into it, she might have it as a gift. The struggle which followed caused Ruby to leave the chamber in order to seek composure. After the screams and laughter subsided, she returned to find that with the aid of several strong hand maidens the queen had succeeded all right in getting the girdle on. Ruby said that the queen could not breathe and that her tongue hung out, but she was pleased, for she had obtained the desired effect—in her own mind at least.

Another interesting example of the strict enforcement of *purdah* is the case of Saleh, the son of a wealthy Moslem merchant. While attending a university in the United States he married an attractive American classmate. After completing their studies, the demands of family and business caused the young couple to visit Jidda, hoping that their visit need not be extended to permanent residence.

Several brothers, as well as Saleh's father, all lived together in a very large house. The various wives of these men formed quite a numerous harem. The American bride was obliged to enter and remain in this harem, in constant association with women who knew not a word of English and with whom she had no common bond except that of being a female. She longed to meet her own countrymen and to speak her own language with others beside her husband. As time passed and their visit extended, any small event would have been a welcome diversion. The girl naturally married with a realization of what marriage to a Moslem entailed should they ever live in a Moslem country, but she did at least have Saleh's assurance that he would never take other wives.

After several months, circumstances at last permitted Saleh to invite a number of Americans to meet his bride in the privacy of a servantless buffet dinner party. Servants would have reported the matter all over town. We were just as anxious in our way to meet her also, and to see what kind of a girl possessed enough courage to accept the role she had chosen. We found her to be an average American, quite pretty and well educated. Needless to say, she was very thrilled to meet other Americans. The occasion meant much more than can possibly be imagined. It was obvious that outside the extreme boredom, she had contracted no lasting regrets.

Fortunately this incident never became known, and the final reward for patience and tolerance was Saleh's appointment by Ibn Saud as one of the Saudi delegates to the United Nations.

Saudi Arabia is governed by Sharia, or Koranic law administered by the complete autocracy of the king. This law permits a man four wives, the number possessed by many who can afford them. Except in homes of the more wealthy where education and the assimilation of modern, democratic ideas permit women a little more latitude and consideration, these oppressed humans are relegated by time, custom and religion to a destiny usually more lacking in dignity, scope and independence than the lot of a slave. Rarely is one literate, even if printed matter should be available. As musical instruments are prohibited, they are denied all avenues of amusement or information. Under such circumstances their only pastime is of necessity confined to eating, gossiping and perhaps the performance of simple tasks like needlework; for their seclusion affords them little opportunity for interest in anything beyond their couch. Thrown upon the limited resources of their own uninstructed minds, there remains but one natural topic of conversation for these unimaginative souls, the subject which covers their only apparent purpose on earth, the breeding and birthing of sons. This sole duty seems confirmed by the attitude of their men who, as so correctly described by Lawrence, "regard our comic reproductive processes not as an unhygienic pleasure, but as the main business of life."

When one considers how sternly the customs of *purdah* are enforced, the Takruni women in the streets exemplified a most incongruous aspect of its zealous application. These women represented many different tribes from Africa, and quite a picturesque colony of them existed outside the city wall. They lived in conical thatched huts and were known as the scavengers of the holy land, for they considered everything as edible which could be chewed and swallowed.

We were not expected to look toward the covered harem windows, and certainly not toward any Arab female figure should one chance to be on the street. She would be so thoroughly covered that not even a slit was left for her eyes, but little gauze blinds provided instead. However, that made no difference. It would have been rude, impertinent and cause for violence to glance at her. But on the other hand, we could observe with humor, yet also with a sense of the inexplicable tragedy of life, the black Takruni women, with faces covered but breasts completely bare, as they sat in the street sifting the dust and camel droppings for the few bits of spilled grain which might have been overlooked by the scavenging goats.

Occasionally one or two of the British or American women made social calls on the harems of various prominent Jiddawis. Although several of them were capable of conversing with these women in Arabic, they found an embarrassing scarcity of mutual subject-ground on which to meet. Had they lacked the ability to speak Arabic they would have been rendered completely mute, and the call reduced to simply sitting and looking at one another.

When a call was paid, the Arab women were usually dressed in their conception of Paris evening gowns, unveiled and heavily embellished by Oriental jewelry and ropes of genuine pearls. Some wives were said to be quite lovely while still young; especially those of Indian, Javanese, Caucasian or Circassian strain. They entertained by serving tea, showing off their numerous children and indulging in local gossip. They displayed little interest in matters outside their own bounded horizon, except as it related to their cramped view of women, the servants of men. Because of their degraded position in life, their minds soon reverted to the only subject known, and they would proceed to ply the visitor with all sorts of questions regarding human behavior in the outside world. They were intrigued with the freedom of their non-Moslem sisters and, as a normal reaction, speculated considerably on the amount of immorality such freedom must naturally engender.

The British Legation, in pursuit of friendly propaganda, once succeeded in showing an educational film for Moslem women upon the legation roof. Many Arabs of the opposite sex, not wanting to miss anything, forbidden or not, seated themselves on the city wall that skirted a lagoon as it passed the legation. From the wall they could view the film at a distance. As an illustration of the quality of these bondaged minds, an innocent scene developed in the picture where a man and a woman were alone in a bedroom. There was an audible gasp from the assembled female audience, for from their experience they believed that if a couple were ever alone there could be but one purpose in the situation or but one result.

The simple situation so excited the imagination of the watching men, however, that many lost their balance in delivering subtle-meaning but healthy elbow jabs among themselves. The shaky old wall finally gave way and every last sensualist landed with a splash in the shallow waters of the dark lagoon. That was the last of educational films.

CHAPTER SEVEN

Donald and Ana meskeen

OUR number was increased about this time by the arrival of another British major named Pat. His wife also arrived several weeks later to pay us a short visit from her war job in Cairo. She belonged to a British women's organization called the F.A.N.N.Y.S. and although it was always good for a joke, I've forgotten what it means.

Eleanor made the eighth white woman in Jidda. She was as attractive as any matronly English woman could be, although the only qualifications necessary to make her extremely popular in Jidda were that she be white and female.

It seems that Eleanor had been a ballet dancer until added girth made such a vocation difficult. She had, however, transmitted some of her passion for dancing to Pat. Their dancing was of the interpretive brand, and a sudden inspiration was liable to hit either one of them while in the act of washing, dressing or simply walking across a room. If unaccustomed to their actions, one would wonder on seeing them, unexpectedly taken by the spirit, to suddenly freeze into a classical pose or as suddenly perform abandoned leaps and spins. They raced and danced on the beach like possessed dervishes and even in their room played games like carefree children. I often spied Eleanor dancing for Pat on the moonlit balcony, dressed as though ready for bed.

When Eleanor first arrived, a loud crash was heard to echo from their room in the middle of the night. The next morning, in determining the cause for hammering, I found Pat and Bukr trying to nail Pat's old bed back together from its collapsed position on the floor.

It was awfully good to see the touch of a woman around, even though it resulted in destruction of the furniture. Pat and Eleanor were both gay and refreshing and their arrival imbued the entire colony with new spirit. They were decidedly British but without the usual inhibited manners; and extroverts in that they were able to find such joyful release and keen pleasures within the limited bounds of Jidda.

Pat had thin blond hair, very round blue eyes and a real *pucka* mustache. He was average in height and had a good start on a stomach, aided by his beer ration. The British army never succeeded in teaching him to stand correctly. He stood as he pleased, in relaxed unmilitary curves. The fullness of his rear supported his trousers but they in turn did a poor job of supporting his stomach. However, Pat did not give a sloppy appearance, only a comfortable one. Like an Arab, he was unique enough to dress comfortably and to be himself at all times.

Eleanor assumed the responsibilities of the kitchen while visiting us. We never knew how she and Hamid managed to understand each other but whatever the method, it resulted in our food becoming almost edible. At least with Eleanor's management and my generous use of DDT, it was possible to eat bread that was reasonably free of weevils. John claimed he missed them, as well as the mouse-droppings in the tea and brown sugar, but then, like the Takarina, John would have eaten anything he could overtake.

If only we could have done something about the flies, for in Arabia they, more than mosquitoes, were the major pest. We had no screens nor netting, so could not control them. I kept Zaid busy with a spray gun but they were replaced by clouds of newcomers from outside as fast as he could slay them. It was especially annoying during the *Hajj* (pilgrimage) when thousands of pilgrims moved through the city. As there were no public conveniences, the flies multiplied overnight on the filth of the streets.

Like the Egyptian flies, their Arabian cousins had the diabolical capacity for driving us mad. They were motivated by purpose and malice aforethought, recognized by the fact that they always made a beeline for one's nose or ears, into which orifices they climbed with the agility of a hound-chased rabbit entering its burrow. They stuck to one, crawling and wiping their dirty feet, and had to be physically removed. It was necessary to fight these satanic insects constantly while dining, carrying the food to the mouth with one hand while shooing them off with the other. Even so, John once ate a fly; at least he insisted that he did, and of course we all believed him.

The first time I inspected the kitchen I found everything black with these crawling pests, including a chicken which Hamid had cleaned for dinner. I could not determine what it was until I shook it, dislodging the covering of flies. Hamid's usual *maleesh* prompted me to throw an accomplished African *vex* which disturbed him not at all. The cloth he produced at my raving, with which to cover the bird, would have contaminated any food it contacted.

Kitchen cloths served every purpose, from drying dishes to mopping the sweat which poured down Hamid's black face. I tore up several shirts for kitchen cloths until some could be secured from Cairo. I first obtained a batch of textile samples but found the servants appropriated them for the making of new *galabiyas*. In the end I was forced to give the matter up, already submissive enough to add my tired *maleesh* to that of Hamid's. On reaching this decision, I retreated from the kitchen, determined never to go there again, hoping that in the future, what I did not know would not hurt me.

When Eleanor returned to Egypt she left Pat, as compensation, a *saluki* pup which she obtained from a desert tribe who raised them for hunting.

The *saluki* goes back to antiquity and resembles a greyhound. *Salukis* are swift in racing but completely lacking in intelligence. As they are also nervous and highstrung, it is impossible to teach them anything except chasing gazelles, an instinct natural to their hunting nature. We viewed Pat's dog with a skeptical eye, realizing our difficulties were laid before us with two gazelles in the house. I had freed the grown ones but an Arab friend had sent Donald a little playmate which he disdainfully ignored. I intended, therefore, to liberate her as well, after she had grown old enough to care for herself.

In naming Pat's dog the servants displayed unsuspected perception, as well as humor, by suggesting *"Ana meskeen,"* which means "I am poor." It was so entirely appropriate that we accepted it and called her *"Ana"* for short.

Ana promptly adopted the stalking method to destroy or worry Donald into an early gazelle heaven. Repeated punishment failed to discourage her. She only screamed madly to make Pat think I was murdering her and even then was quite prepared to do it all over again. So we awaited a tragedy. Donald would not run if he saw Ana, but instead turned to butt in determined indignation until she retreated or someone separated them. However, if the dog silently stole upon Donald, her quick rush so frightened him that he fled in terror as a natural reaction. In such panic he was apt to leap through a window or off the terrace, a possibility that kept us all alert.

Fred was once resting on the sofa when Donald, pursued by Ana, leaped over him for the open window. Fred awoke just in time to grab him by a hind leg and haul him back to doubtful safety. When he ran to me, chased by Ana, I scolded him for running, but he only rolled his cud reflectively, flipped his tail and dismissed the matter.

Fred's bed was beside a window that opened onto the front terrace and his door opened onto a hall leading into the living room. The living room in turn led to the same terrace, so that an animal racetrack could easily be made of the layout. Doors and windows could not be closed without danger of suffocation, consequently our livestock could not be locked into separate sleeping quarters with their respective owners.

With the threat of Ana, Donald would not venture from my room during the night—and Ana was afraid to enter—but while I was away on a trip to Cairo, Donald was obliged to adopt Fred as a sleeping companion and protector during my absence. This exposed him to a certain amount of danger, however, for the dogs were also welcome in Fred's room. In fact they usually made it their sleeping quarters. Mesco, the big *pariah,* was only an overgrown puppy, clumsy and friendly with a heart full of love for Donald. Nevertheless, he was not above entering into a chase already begun.

I learned that while I was away all animal relations remained peaceful and friendly during the daytime only. They usually waited until the household was asleep before starting the chase, and Ana always started it. Round and round they went, a gazelle then a dog, another gazelle then another dog, until it must have been a question of who was chasing whom. They leaped through the window into Fred's room, clearing the bed where he lay sleeping, out his door, into the living room, onto the terrace and through the window again, sliding at every curve on the glazed tile and piling up rugs until someone awoke and put a stop to it.

When I returned from Cairo I noticed that Fred's mosquito netting was removed and asked the reason. He told me that in one of the animals' nocturnal chases someone failed to clear the net. This resulted in two dogs and two gazelles landing in a complex scramble atop his sleeping figure. On finally extricating himself and restoring order, he decided the most logical thing to do was to remove the racetrack obstacle. Although the yelping dogs must have proved distracting I nevertheless presume it was somewhat like counting sheep after that, as they sailed unobstructed over his reclining figure.

The feud between Donald and Ana finally reached a stage where the household became divided into two opposing factions. It was a case of Donald, backed by the servants and two Americans, opposing Ana and the British members. Mesco belonged in both camps, but this was caused by his affection for Donald as well as his love for the chase. He meant no harm and doubtless acted under Ana's influence.

Just when it seemed we would sever all diplomatic relations, Ana considerately disappeared. She was never heard of again. The servants all maintained their innocence in the matter, but since she stubbornly refused to be house-broken and they had no liking for cleaning up after a dog, they remained subject to a certain amount of suspicion. I personally refrained from any investigation. Whatever the medium, I felt only too relieved with the solving of the problem of "Donald vs. *Ana meskeen.*"

CHAPTER EIGHT

By the Grace of Allah

Our telephone system had been ingeniously contrived, along with the climate, to drive man to an early grave. It was a very limited system and extended only between the various legations, government offices and a few merchants. Ahmed, our interpreter, was unqualified to make my calls for me, as he should have done, for the only reason that he could not shout loud enough. If I desired to contact the American Legation, for example, I soon learned not to assume the labor involved myself, but to set Bukr the task of cranking the infernal instrument instead.

Every servant possessed at least one redeeming quality, and this was Bukr's, for only he seemed capable of any success whatever with the telephone. He cranked the thing until his arm became tired, lifting the receiver after each long crank to shout, *"NOM? NOM?"* (yes, yes) into the mouthpiece. There was seldom an answering *"Nom?"* so he hung up to repeat the performance. When the ringing and shouting got on my nerves I dispatched Zaid to the central switchboard, located in the post office, and within shouting distance itself, conveying a request that the operator answer our ring.

Zaid usually found the operator sipping Turkish coffee or Arab mint tea, unmindful of the ringing, should the system be operating that far, and demanded an immediate connection with the legation. Bukr, on our end, finally became connected with Beit Americani! After much shouting of *"NOM? NOM?"* during which it was necessary for Bukr to gesture wildly as if the connection were visual as well as oral, I concluded that Beit Americani had stated that *they* were trying to get the American Legation and "what the hell were we doing on the line?"

This meant hanging up and starting from the beginning again—a good form of forced exercise for both Bukr and Zaid. After Zaid trotted back across the square again our next success turned out to be Gellatly Hankey, the British shipping agent. In anger they claimed to have been trying to get us all morning and, "why in the name of Allah the Merciful didn't we answer our phone?"

Their business disposed of, we started again, as I sat close by, thoroughly engrossed in such a fascinating game of chance. At this stage Bukr removed his tarbush and mopped his brow. He was often obliged to lay the receiver down so that he might be free to gesture with both hands, while beads of sweat poured from his forehead. I envisioned the owner of the voice on the other end doing the same thing, neither of them hearing what the other said but each working himself close toward apoplexy.

By this time all work in the office came to a standstill, everyone either anxious to know what might be the next development or else threatening a nervous breakdown. I was always anxious to continue, wondering if we might not somehow get the king himself on the line. However, for the sake of others' sanity and before Bukr should remove his *galabiya,* I scribbled a chit and assigned Zaid the task of carrying it across town to the legation. If he wore a tarbush the chit was carried beneath it, for Zaid, like all of his race, seemed unable to move unless both hands were completely free. He brought back a reply in seven minutes flat, causing me to vow that whenever in a hurry I would simply send a note or go in person.

The history of the telephone in Arabia provides a vivid example of the difficulties and opposition encountered by Ibn Saud in his early program to unite and improve the lot of his Bedouin people. The program conceived by him was the result of his life's study of a backward country that suddenly found itself in a small and modern world. He was perhaps the only one who realized that what had been adequate in the past for a people isolated from the world by the barriers of sea and desert was not desirable under the demands of the twentieth century. The first essential in his program was the abolition of tribal warfare and the uniting of all the many tribes into one peaceful and stable nation. This he finally accomplished for the first time in Arabia's history, and is in itself a long and fascinating story.

Ibn Saud planned religious reform, gradual modernization and the introduction of new administrative and educational ideas. Religious reform was conspicuously imperative but such reform was far from acceptable to the stern and fanatical religious leaders and their followers, nor was it popular with the more prosperous but less orthodox class. The institution of his reforms proved to be a long and patient process, but fortunately for his country, Ibn Saud was born a leader, possessing all the personal qualities necessary for success. He had vision and intellect, religious zeal and political keenness, but above all, the courage and determination to pursue his plans.

There are approximately 230 million Moslems in the world, or one-seventh of the world's population. Moslem sectarianism in general is virtually negligible, except for a fundamental division into Sunnites and Shiites. The Sunnite sect is considered as the norm because of its vast superiority of numbers; while the Shiite sect of perhaps fifty million have departed in many ways from Moslem orthodoxy. The Sunnites derive their name from the Sunna, which supplements the Koran. It is fundamental in Islam and is made up of collections of traditions, moral sayings and anecdotes of the Prophet Mohammed, sifted and collected with unflagging effort by men from the earliest times. It is almost as important as the Koran itself, the most influential book in the world after the Bible, for in the Sunna lie all the elaborations of Koranic teaching essential to the firm establishment of a world religion. So little of the Koran is dogmatic or legalistic that early in the history of Islam, Moslems found it inadequate as an authority for their way of life.

Islam has been given its catholicity of view, its constant unity with the past and its continuous flexibility by yet another supplement to the Koran, the Ijma, which is a collection of principles as expressed in the most important sayings of the Prophet.

Thus there are three foundations for Islam; the sacred Koran or divine word as revealed to Mohammed, and established as the canonical text in 651 A.D., supplemented by the Sunna and the Ijma.

The two major branches of Sunnites and Shiites are both divided politically into many groups and countless sects, the Wahhabi being the only important modern branch of the Sunnites. The Wahhabis might be described in Western terms as puritanical fundamentalists. The principles of their creed are interpreted by a fanatical and powerful group of church elders learned in Moslem theology and law, called the *ulema*. This body of men exert a tremendous influence on the mentality and behavior of their sect. It has been the *ulema* and its followers which has deterred and opposed the king in all of his reforms and innovations. One might think that with his absolute power Ibn Saud, a Wahhabi himself, could proceed boldly regardless of the attitude of the *ulema,* but because of the great power wielded by them, it has always been necessary to secure their conversion to a new idea first and to seek their co-operation before ever attempting to put it into operation. Furthermore, it has been necessary for the king to exercise the greatest care in keeping his own life and actions above cause for the *ulema*'s criticism.

The *ulema*'s interpretation of Wahhabism does not permit adoration of saints or veneration of monuments and graves. They permit nothing to stand between man and God. Music, the arts, silken clothes, alcohol and tobacco are among the things forbidden. Nothing which pleases the senses is allowed to weaken the Wahhabi's religious ardor and only the most orthodox doctrines are accepted in their interpretations.

From the time he first came into power, Ibn Saud has had this fanatical group to deal with. He has had to preserve their confidence and confer with them on all matters since they are responsible for carrying out the religious laws of the land. Under them come all the religious officials, the *mueddins* (*muezzins*), *mutawas* (preachers) religious instructors and keepers of the mosques. The *ulema* would have raised the country against Ibn Saud if at any time they could have proven that he deviated from their own concepts. Although the king is an extremely religious man, the *ulema* have always been suspicious and alert for the slightest excuse to charge him with wandering from their strict code. It is the natural code of a people of their background, and by necessity it replaces all the unattainable joys of existence.

When the king had the first telephone installed he met with the usual objection on the part of the *ulema*. They posed the dubious claim that such mechanisms were not permitted by the teachings of the Prophet, although it is very doubtful if Mohammed ever visualized such inventions. They clearly realized that any modernization whatever would lead to secularism and materialism, both of which are opposed to their creed. In the end Ibn Saud was forced to remove the telephone.

As time went on, step by step, by means of education, flattery and even ruthlessness, he led the *ulema,* and with them the Wahhabi masses, to more advanced conceptions both of the world and of their own religion. Only by patiently widening their horizon and persuading them of the necessity as well as the desirability of improvements, could he reach his goal. He has succeeded in gradually overcoming the opposition of the *ulema* on all major issues.

As for the telephone, Ibn Saud eventually persuaded the *ulema* that if Allah did not wish the mechanism to be used, it simply would not function. Moreover, if it were evil, it could not carry the words of the Koran over it. The *ulema* finally agreed that if the Holy Word could be heard over the wires, they would accept this as a sign that Allah approved.

Arrangements for the test were made and of course it worked, with the result that there are telephones of questionable performance in Arabia today. But I often thought, when trying to make them operate, of the king's courage and of the extreme risk he ran; for that he ever obtained his first connection was indeed "by the Grace of Allah!"

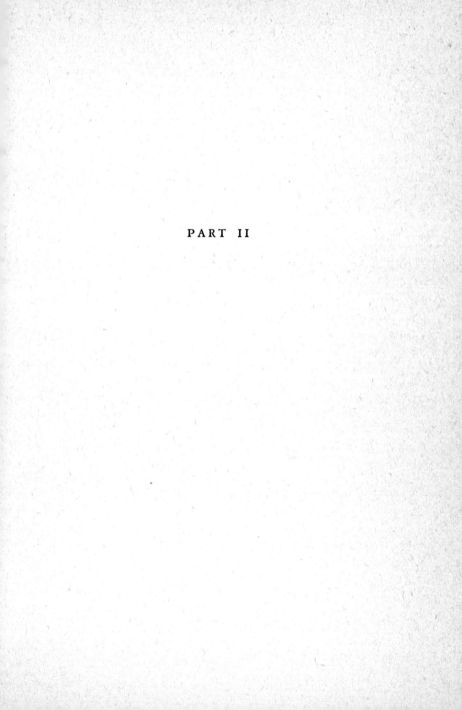

PART II

His Majesty, Abdul Aziz Ibn Abdur-Rahman, Al Faisal
Al Saud, Prince of the Faithful and Lord of Arabia (seated),
and his son Saud al Saud, Crown Prince and heir-apparent
to the throne (standing), pictured in the palace at Riyadh.

Street scene in Jeddah

Street scene in old Jeddah

Proud of his many sons, King Ibn Saud is pictured here with 19 of them on the palace roof at Riyadh. Some of the older sons assist him in governmental affairs.

We finally settled on "Donald" which Fred thought also absurd.

A typical Arab house in Jeddah. This was the original office
of the Arabian American Oil Company.

A captured viper held in a noose on the desert in Saudi
Arabia. These snakes are related to American rattlers.

Aerial view of an 'ain' at Al Kharj

View of Suq at Saudi Arabia's capital city of Riyadh.

The congregation in the Great Mosque of Mecca dispersing after prayers round the Ka'ba.

Thousands of tents crowd the plains between Medina and Mecca where pilgrims live during the pilgrimages.

CHAPTER NINE

Salaam Alaikum or Farewell to Jidda

It MAY have been springtime somewhere, but not in Arabia, at the time when it became necessary for me to make the long trip across the Arabian Peninsula to the Najd. We had an agricultural mission over toward the Persian Gulf at a place called Al Kharj, fifty miles south of Riyadh, the Najd capital where the king usually resides. The purpose of my trip was conveyed to His Majesty through proper diplomatic channels, and his necessary permission received. Whether this meant he would receive me, I did not know, although I hoped he would. It is his custom to grant audience to anyone making the long journey, since they are either traveling on invitation or by special permission for official reasons.

Pat willingly agreed to accompany me and I was glad, for with him along I knew the trip would be an exciting, memorable adventure. Pat was always in good humor, of steady disposition and prejudiced toward nothing. He liked adventure and easily adapted himself to any situation, being especially at ease with the Arabs.

We called on His Excellency, Sheikh Abdullah al Sulaiman, the Minister of Finance, to discuss details of the proposed trip. The minister received us warmly once admitted to his presence, and seated us in big gilt chairs which seemed alien to the Arab setting. Sheikh Abdullah was a kind, elderly little man, so unassuming that one might easily misjudge the extent of his power and prestige.

While we amiably drank hot mint tea, all details of the trip were quickly arranged through an interpreter. Sheikh Abdullah promised to send us one of his most trusted guards, a guide and a driver. All official angles would be in his hands, and we knew how our progress and welfare would be flashed to his office by the Saudi police stations scattered at great intervals along the way and that he in turn would keep the king advised. To the king, a foreigner's every move is always known.

Bukr brought in a package that evening from the minister which we found to contain complete Arab outfits for both Pat and myself. We realized it to be not only a gracious gesture but an open hint as to our dress, should we be received at the palace in Riyadh. We intended to wear khaki across country, only observing the customs so far as headdress was concerned. The Arab headdress, or *qhotra*, is not only a protection in passing through tribes of desert nomads, but serves as relief from sun, wind and sand.

An Arab tailor was summoned from the bazaars and we modeled

the gowns standing on stools while he made adjustments to their length. Pat looked as ridiculous as I felt. He stood stiffly on the stool as though waiting to be shot through the air by the prick of the tailor's needle. His blue eyes were more round than ever, as though surprised at the indignity being perpetrated below. Dickie and John sat around making subtle but caustic remarks as if at a fashion show and the grinning servants crowded the door to see what manner of Arabs we would make.

The undergarment, or *thob,* is a long white silk gown and over it is worn the *mishlah,* of finely woven transparent camel wool, richly embroidered in deep bands of gold around the neck, across the shoulders and down the open front. One feels very much undressed when wearing such light garments.

We planned to take a command car and a truck to Al Kharj, leaving them there for the mission's use and returning by way of the Persian Gulf if necessary. There we could catch a commercial plane to Cairo and thence to Jidda—quite roundabout, but the only feasible route.

The heavy truck was stocked with barrels of petrol that we could siphon out as needed, two barrels of water, blankets and bed rolls; and most important of all, two metal tracks in ten-foot lengths. Without these we would be unable to take the truck through many sandy spots since it was not equipped with the marvelous mechanism of four-wheel-drive like the command car. Boxes of canned foods, cooking utensils and all the other items required for an eight-hundred-mile desert journey were all stowed in the command car where Pat and I intended to ride. We would relieve each other in driving, with the truck carrying our companions following behind, except in unmarked stretches where it would be necessary to rely on the guide to lead the way.

Our caravan left Jidda early one Tuesday morning and the entire

household turned out to see us off and wish us a good trip, *"insha'*
Allah." Donald stood on the balcony forlornly watching our departure
and I almost decided against my better judgment to take him along.
After making each of the servants swear on the Koran that they would
guard him with their lives, and I in turn threatening to have them all
beheaded if anything happened to him, we self-consciously adjusted
our *qhotras* and *agals* (head ropes), waved good-by and sped off in a
cloud of dust, scattering goats and Arab children.

Following a good dirt road, maintained by the Saudi Arabian
Mining Syndicate (known as SAMS), we headed northeast, crossing
the great sand plain dotted with occasional hummocks, to the ochre-
colored Hijaz hills. This road had been laid out by an American
engineer when he decided to develop the gold mines at Mahd Dhahab,
"the cradle of gold." He claims to have studied old documents dating
back to the second chapter of the Book of Genesis before reopening
the ancient workings, once operated by King Solomon.

Today these mines, located 248 miles deep in the desert, are operated
by American engineers and technicians, using American machinery
and training Arab workmen in the skilled techniques of modern gold
mining. The tailings left by ancient miners were profitably reworked
before the present underground operations were begun. The complexity of the ore permits the production of only oil floatation con-
centrates and cyanide precipitates. The rock, blasted from the earth's
deep interior, is crushed to a gray powder and put through a chemical
process. Water is added to make a wet soup, then the deadly poisonous
sodium cyanide, which dissolves the metals. The liquid containing
the suspended metals is drawn off and put through an evaporation
process which leaves only a residue of dull black dust. Though it is
hard to believe on examination, this dust is composed of all the metals
found in the ore; gold, silver, lead, zinc, iron and copper. It is trans-

ported to huge smelters in the United States as only very extensive plants can separate and recover in marketable form the various metals.

Pat and I decided to follow the mine road for perhaps two hundred miles before branching off into the uncharted desert. The arid country seemed fairly interesting, though wasted and stony, for our path gradually climbed one crest of hills after another, dipping down to wide sandy *wadis* dotted with knolls of Salam trees (acacias) to ascend higher escarpments beyond. After hours of steady driving, the hot dry air seemed to have cooked us alive and our muscles ached with the pain of unaccustomed jolting. So, when cresting a ragged hill we spied a green oasis shimmering in the heat of a feverish valley gorge, we hurried forward with renewed eagerness.

A recent torrential rain had crashed through the ravine in a swirling flood, and a broad rushing stream still followed its bed, edged by welcome green tamarisk and woody acacias. Its cool refreshing beauty drew us irresistibly to a halt and we quickly threw off our hot garments and plunged into the depths of a natural pool trapped by flood-created sand banks. It was impossible to believe we were still in Arabia. Bedouin suddenly appeared from simply nowhere, as they always do, to squat in the white sand and gaze in rather offended fascination at our undignified nakedness. The sense of modesty is exceedingly strong with the Arabs.

After our cooling swim we prepared to eat and to our consternation found that neither the guard, the driver nor the guide had brought food or water for themselves. They had been instructed to do so and had received fifty riyals each as an advance tip with which to purchase supplies. Bedouin, however, consider it a sign of weakness to carry provisions for such a short trip of eight or ten days; and ours found it easier to rely on either Allah or our own hospitality. They refused canned meat, fearful it was pork, and also beans until convinced they were free of meat. With the flour we gave them Hasan, the guard, mixed water and kneaded it into a cake several inches thick and perhaps ten inches across. This he buried in the hot ashes of a brushwood fire. It quickly baked sufficiently to please him and, withdrawing it, he brushed away the clinging ashes and shared it with us all. Ali, our garrulous guide, would accept nothing but the bread and tea and on such fare he lived for the entire crossing.

We forded the stream and bounced on through the insufferable heat of afternoon, following SAMS' road across sand-filled wadis and climbing the rocky skeletons of naked, black granite hills which shone like greased metal. Small herds of fleet gazelle bounded off through the wadi scrub of thorn and yellow-tufted grass like passing heat illusions. Each ascent leveled off into plateaus of boulders that glinted blindingly in the dancing heat and though we descended their steep sides to cross a thorn-scrub field, flaked with porphyry, green schist and granite shale, we climbed still higher and higher. These elevations afforded great sweeps of view, undulating off to towering castlelike buttes and bordering lines of high mesas, straight and level as the precision of nature could form them. Swept by burning breezes like oven blasts, we wrapped our *qhotras* about our faces, leaving only a slit through which to gaze at the glittering wilderness.

We passed the lonely well of Al Birka, where watering goats scattered in mad fright from the roar of our laboring motors. As the red sun gathered to the west we paused at the well of Hadha where several brown huts, bunched together as though for security, seemed lost and miserable upon the desolate landscape.

Hadha is one of a chain of cisterns which date from about 800 A.D. and owe their existence to the piety of Zubaydah Khatum, wife of Baghdad's most famous caliph, Harum el Rashid. It is said that this princess, in making several pilgrimages, dug wells, built cisterns and raised a wall with occasional towers between Baghdad and Mecca to guide pilgrims over the shifting sands.

After our companions dabbed a little water on themselves, as prescribed, and said their evening prayers in unison, we continued a short way until after sunset; although our backs were raw from bouncing and our eyes ached from the glare of light striking up all day at a sharp angle from the silver sand and shining pebbles. At the wells of Sufaina we turned onto open desert and camped in a rugged lava field where only a few stunted juniper scrub grew in stubborn determination. After food and hot coffee comforted our aching bodies we fell upon the bed rolls, unmindful of scorpions or other perils of the night, to gaze in contemplated wonder at the unearthly beauty overhead. The moon was late, so our dark plane extended to the rounded horizon, without life or color, but the atmosphere seemed self-illumined, not capable of penetrating to the earth's dark surface but rising from it, brighter and brighter, until reaching the brilliance of the innumerable stars held in its endless expanse. I lost consciousness somewhere in this great immensity.

As a small portion of the eastern horizon showed a faint light along its edge, we stirred in our still dark beds upon the hard unyielding lava field. The wet, cold dew had bathed my face and transformed my covering wool *bedie* into a diamond blanket which sparkled in the reflecting light of Ali's already dancing fire. My watch indicated the time to be four o'clock "somewhere" so I called, *"Salaam alaikum"* to Pat (Peace be on you), and received a sleepy, *"Wa alaikum essalaam"* in reply (And on you peace).

We stiffly rolled out, made coffee and scrambled eggs on the fiery embers and prepared to push eastward, over unmarked territory, hoping to intercept within fifty miles the road which leads from Mecca to Riyadh. Ali, as the official guide, felt it his privilege to point out the direction, which he assured us was *kwayis tarik* (good road), and insisted upon it. So we followed him just as it became light enough to see, over ragged, blue-black volcanic fields, impassable to anything but our sturdy machines; until we halted, unable to proceed further, in a vast field of huge boulders. Protesting that northward the terrain was passable and *kwayis* we knew that Ali was lost. I demanded to know just where the Riyadh road lay, since he was the guide, and finally forced him to admit *"Allah yi'rif"* (God knows).

Perhaps Ali was right, but that did not help us, and since being lost on the desert seemed a most undesirable way of quitting this earth, Pat and I decided our own course. We managed with much difficulty to turn about, then started to retrace the way around piled basalt blocks until finally turning in a more southeasterly direction. The truck could not always follow where we led, but perforce made its way in our general direction, avoiding the rougher ground which only we could negotiate, speeding on good patches as though frightened of being left behind, and carrying an angry, muttering Ali, flapping in the breeze of the running board. This "show" was supposed to be his and he did not like being done out of it.

Pat was driving, a job which to me required every ounce of energy and attention. Pat, however, held no regard for rough places and applied himself with as little concern as though whizzing down an open boulevard. His headcloth trailed freely in the breeze, threatening to fly off on its own. Turning to me, Pat stroked his spunky-looking mustache thoughtfully. "Bob," he said, "that bloke Ali is no more of a guide than I am!"

This but confirmed my own suspicions. "You're damned right!" bounced from my parched throat. "Maybe he's been to Riyadh many times, but I'd hate to depend on his getting us there."

I brooded over the matter, wondering if we should turn around and thinking of the many long miles, unmarked, ahead of us. We were without a compass and our map would be of little help. With a growing certainty that we would never find the Najd capital, I asked, "What are we going to do?"

"Oh, we'll carry on," Pat said, stepping on the gas in a joy of anticipation. It would not matter to him if we never returned to civilization.

The going became worse and we had continually to circle large fields of basalt until reaching lava fields and cushioned shoulders of black cinders again. Small ancient craters appeared here and there and from them ran spines of broken basalt and granite, making our passage all but impossible. The terrain finally changed from black volcanic, windswept barrens to another imperceptible upward slope, the watershed of the Hijaz. This was of red granite stones and long swells of slate slivers and hornblende schist and was without verdure of any kind.

After many miles of uncertainty the long slope leveled off to great sand plains that skirted around tongues of sun-browned rock ridges, then suddenly we came upon the Mecca-Riyadh trail, worn into the earth and deeply rutted, with brown sand piled up like snowbanks on either side. This was some relief to my anxiety, if we could but follow the trail and not lose it.

Where the sand gave way to shingle areas the trail spread out to the width of fifty or more vehicles, for each passing driver liked to pick his own path when allowable, avoiding the bogs and treacherous ruts of others. Thickets of sickly, dust-laden alkali bushes began to appear with small rounded hills at their bases where they had caught and held the flying sand. An occasional Sidr tree (*Jujuba spina Christi*) further relieved the monotonous landscape. By now the sun had become as racking as can be conceived, so, already sore from perpetual bouncing, we stopped to eat on the clean wind-brushed sand under a few aged Sidrs and listened to Ali boast, as he fluffed his bandit beard, that he had known the way all the time.

Lunch over, we continued our hot and dusty way. The heat began to move in waves upon us so that we recoiled as though trying to dodge blasts from an open oven and kept passing the water canteen back and forth between us. The radiator water reached a temperature of 210° Fahrenheit and the steering wheel became too hot to handle with the naked hand. I found that wetting my *qhotra* and winding it about my head and face afforded a short relief until it quickly dried and had to be wetted again. The use of camphor ice soothed our cracked lips but nothing could ease the shock and pounding produced by the corrugated tracks which led over a continuing featureless plain of rutted sand and sun-burnt flints. We passed no signs of life all day, no travelers or Bedawi; not even gazelles, birds or lizards in that ominous land which seemed incapable of life and hostile even to its passing.

Continuous fighting with the almost unmanageable wheel soon fatigued us but we changed places as one or the other wearied, until near sundown when the approach of a rolling, reddish-yellow formation of wind-borne sand to the north threatened to intercept us. As its onslaught became imminent we halted near some acacias and quickly fastened on the car curtains. The air became hazy with dust swept down from the Nefudh, the great sand desert of Northern Arabia, and the wind increased in a whirling force. Before we were ready for it, stinging sand particles began to graze and pain our already inflamed faces. As we dove into the car the heat contained in the *simoom* enveloped us in its fiery intensity, causing the trickling sweat to feel cool. The sand-filled wind rushed with a steady long moan, to rock

and beat our heavy vehicle in a growing roar of flying sand and uprooted bushes.

Huddling in the back of the car, I shouted to Pat, asking what he
would give for a good drink and he, gasping, shouted back to ask if
I were kidding. The orange light had deepened with the full force of
the storm, but not so much as to prevent my finding a bottle of Johnny
Walker tucked in my bag, which I had been saving for just such a
time. Pat could hardly believe his senses as I thrust the bottle into
his hands. While the wind howled over us we raised our veiling
qhotras to wash the gritty dust down parched throats with Scotch-
rinses. In our slightly dehydrated condition it produced the immediate
effect of extreme lassitude and Pat began to sing tipsily,

> "To market, to market, with my brother Jim,
> When somebody flung a tomater at him!
> Tomaters' all right when they come in a skin,
> But this bastard didn't, it come in a tin!"

We felt foolishly happy, as if there were no one else in the world,
just we two and the wild elements. When they abated we stepped out
to brush the grime from our faces and shake it from our clothes and
luggage. The dust had entered through small cracks to form irregular
piles on the car floor, and had even crept into tightly closed bags.

We fixed a cold dinner from the improvised kitchenette which
opened by dropping the tailgate; then, since it was already quite dark
and turning cold, we rolled out our bed rolls right where we stood and
contentedly crawled into them. Hasan, our tall dark Najd guard,
threw a heavy *bedie* (woolen cloak of the Bedou) about him and
said he would sit near us during the night, for it was a wild country
and we had not pulled far from the trail. Though we were totally

unconcerned, he, however, felt charged with the responsibility for our safety.

Hasan was very quiet and reserved, but he instilled a feeling of confidence in us. He was dressed in a long black *abaya* and was well fortified with a heavy rifle. Two handsome daggers, sheathed in the intricate beauty of Yemeni silverwork, were worn tucked beneath his cartridge belt. He spoke a "peace upon us" as the intense loneliness of this far and desolate place settled like the night dampness. The pain of the day's heat and struggle had so worn us that I quickly drifted off into a solid sleep.

CHAPTER TEN

Only Space, and God

THE chilling cry of a hyena awakened me to quick consciousness and I found Hasan still beside us. It would not be long until light, so I snuggled a bit between the woolly smoothness of my heavy *bedie* while Hasan dug a small pit and built a fire from wind-blown desert twigs. He started the blaze with a match, then deftly covered the pile with his *qhotra* to protect it from any wind, while blowing upon the feeble flame. When it grew enough to be comforting in the morning chill, we arose. Pat packed the gear while I fried some bacon which sent out such delicious aroma on the morning mist that even Hasan looked tempted. I coaxed him to have some but he cracked a sad smile and said, *"la, la, mush kwayis,"* meaning no, it was not good for him. The can of Maxwell House coffee sitting in the sand, a million miles (it seemed) from home, looked so implausible that Pat and I both decided it was good subject material for a photograph. When it became light enough Pat snapped me stoking the fire with the coffee can beside me and laughingly suggested it might be worth something to General Foods to possess the negative.

We started off just as the sun peeped over the horizon, flooding its rays almost level with the surface and casting long, extended and sharply defined shadows from even the smallest ground irregularities. These shadows contracted as the sun rose higher, as though melting in toward the dawn, until the sun's rays crested their parent ridges, snuffing them out altogether here and there, one by one, until the very last was finally extinguished. The increasingly vigorous sun then seemed to concentrate on trying to blind us as we attempted to cross its conquered territory.

Early in the morning we passed the brackish wells of Al Qathma, and only stopped to say, *"Sabah al-heir"* ("May your morning be bright") to the Bedouin watering their camels and to receive their return, *"Sabah an-nour."* The wells were holes in the level ground and the water was drawn up in skin buckets. Although these desert nomads offered us some, we politely refused for it was evident the water was fouled by the slow return trickle from the mud of spilt water and camel urine.

We covered many monotonous miles in the early hours, over deeply rutted tracks that occasionally ascended above the sand levels to long inclines of harder elements of flint and varieties of amphibolic rock. The trail finally topped a spiny ridge of pure-white flint. A slow descent followed over the same formation with outcroppings of quartz, ending in beds of churned white sand that for miles across looked like the battlefield of giant prehistoric monsters. If Pat were driving when we hit such areas, I aided in his strenuous efforts by putting in the four-wheel-shift just when we felt our whirling wheels to be losing their traction. It felt like battling the wild waves of a sea as I leaned ready to throw the gear when he yelled, "NOW!" Then we could feel the car steady itself by the added effort of two more pulling wheels and doggedly continue in a shifting, wobbling course across the blinding whiteness.

On gaining the safety of harder ground we stopped to breathe and mop our grimy faces while watching the truck fighting for its life and kicking up a miniature blizzard in its wake. Its whine increased to a roar as it slowed, then suddenly gave up and settled with a grunt. Pat and I staggered back, each carrying a steel track to rescue our hot, streaming Arabs by digging the wheels free and placing the tracks before them. We ceased to count the times it lost in its struggles, but there were harder times still ahead.

A stop was made for lunch on a great plain void of all except pebbled swells of glassy sand dotted with scraggly Sidr scrub which danced in the visible heat waves caused by the ever-burning sun in an always cloudless sky. The elevation here was perhaps only four thousand feet, but because of the tremendous expanse of naked waste, stretching off into the infinite haze of distance, we possessed the feeling of being on top of the world with everything else seeming to lie somewhere lower in the impenetrable beyond.

Sometime in the afternoon Abraqiya appeared in the wide Wadi el Miyah. As we loudly approached the small oasis, a string of knee-haltered camels jumped up clumsily and hobbled about grotesquely on three legs while their Bedawi masters chased after them to hang onto their halters in a quieting attempt. The well was surrounded by nomads and their goats. A few date palms cast a lacework of filtered shade to the dusty floor and to the tiny plots of watered green *dhurra* beyond. The traveler who comes out of such desolate wadis to rest his heated motor, or to couch his camel where water has brought a little greenness and beauty, will never wonder what heaven is like.

Before sunset we reached a ruined sandstone land, followed on a higher level by old volcanic fields, then dropping to outcroppings of red sandstone again. Supper was eaten early because we could not resist stopping in the shaded protection of a high, rounded wall of irregular red sandstone. Its floor was a carpet of soft, fine red sand, swirled here and there by the wind when trapped in this natural bowl. It seemed a cozy nook, cutting off the open expanse of desert and affording us a smaller world which might be comprehended.

Scampering lizards caused loose pieces of stone to rattle downward as they fled beyond sight. Realizing themselves to be unharmed they later returned to a point where they could peer with beady eyes at the noisy intruders, while breathing their yellow throats excitedly in and out.

The pervading peace of the spot caused us to tarry and rest and finally to camp for the night. As the increasing darkness robbed the formations of their passionate reds and yellows and finally turned them into only black outlines, Ali built a fire of thorny brushwood round which Pat and I laid on our blankets to talk and watch the eastern sky become light by the unseen but rising moon. It soon appeared, moving in noticeable rises and in an immensity of orange light and a nearness unnoticed before. It transformed the stark landscape into inanimate beauty, producing the effect where the Arab, more than most people, is conscious and willing to talk of their ever-present God. Those who spend enough time in the desert to forget its loneliness and its void gradually gain an increasing awareness of God and His meaning. The Arabs speak of these open wastes as places where nothing is—except God.

We awoke the next morning to find ourselves covered with locusts.

They had flown in during the night, probably migrating to other pastures, and we were doubtless the most edible looking things in the vast expanse they had traversed. The ground was alive with them, our blankets covered, and though stiff with cold they were nevertheless trying to eat everything including the rubber tires of our vehicles. As I approached the nearest wheel to watch their efforts, one gripped the tire with all four feet and kept his eyes warily upon me while trying to bite greedily into the rubber. Ali and Hasan scooped up a great quantity and roasted them in a large covered pan over the embers. They, as well as Pat, enjoyed cracking and munching on roasted hoppers, declaring them a delicacy.

We left our snug shelter as soon as possible but hoppers turned up in our gear and in car corners and compartments for days after. Following the same grind as the day before, we decided that at least half the distance to Riyadh had been covered, if not more, and considered it good traveling to make four hundred miles in three days. Everyone had said a hundred miles daily would be more than good, but the distance had seemed so impressive, once on the desert, that we felt without driving ten or more hours each day, Riyadh might never be reached.

We passed the well of Khanuqa where black and white fat-tailed sheep were being watered. The strong Bedouin women, looking like witch doctors, ceased hauling up their dripping goatskin buckets to stare at us. They wore the usual black veils trimmed in red, heavily hung with a wealth of gold coins. None of us spoke to them for there is no greeting between men and women in Arabia.

The track began a sharp descent, winding back and forth to avoid the serrated outcroppings of slate that snaked north and south, washed bare by countless centuries of wind and rain. Ahead lay the unlimitable downhill sweep of a great valley, modulating into the distance and dotted thickly with alkali bushes and clumps of *tamarindi* (tamarisk trees) extending to high red and brown cliffs on the veiled horizon. From our map we realized this to be a descent from the central Arabian plateau, to the slightly lower highlands of the Najd.

The central floor of the valley was flecked with pools of glassy surfaced water caused by recent rains. From here the cliffs looked no closer whatever, but at their bases appeared thin layers of mist, streaked as though applied with a brush. Southward where the cliffs gave way to plain again a patch of blue sky appeared above the horizon between two streaks of mist, and floating in the upper layer was a scene of stately palm groves. We thought it odd that such stretches of palms would be growing apparently on the high edge of distant cliffs, but with our progress the scene shifted and we realized it to be a mirage and not just a product of fevered minds.

We detoured the reddish pools, avoiding the thick red mud as much as possible, for here and there was evidence of a daring, if not foolish, driver having attempted to cross. The mud was torn up into great furrows, the old tracks filled perilously with scummy water. In places it seemed that passing vehicles had plowed themselves so deeply they must have disappeared into the earth. The threat of these bogs was frightening and we gave them wide berth. Edges of pools were scaled to the appearance of crocodile hide. Evaporation and drying had cracked the mud into tesseraed mosaic patterns but we knew their appearance was deceptive and that under the artistic crust lay mud so slippery as to throw a camel.

The valley became less scarred with motor tracks as we began to climb again to sandier and then rockier ground, finally disappearing altogether where the terrain became so hard and stony as to defy the imprint of tires. With the disappearance of the trail we became uncertain and waited for the truck to catch up so that Ali could be consulted. To assert himself he perversely suggested a direction that we all agreed was far astray. We overruled him despite his angry beard-pulling and wild gestures and set out with the suggestion that he could go in whatever direction he pleased, but we would, with reason, bear northeast toward a gap in the ridges. It provoked such anger in Ali that he retained a bitter mood all day. When we stopped to rest he remained silent, sitting apart, tugging at his beard and muttering into it. I hardly knew if he were praying or swearing but I did begin to wonder if he were not working on some plot of his own.

Our progress, however, proved our deductions and sense of direction to be correct, for we soon came upon the trail again where it twisted through a rocky gorge cut into crazy layers of sandstone that formed the great ridge seen earlier in the day.

Tamarisk trees had withstood the rush of flood waters down the stairlike dry waterbed and edged its higher sides. The easterly descending gorge widened into a sandy wadi with a scattered confusion of islands and pinnacles of sandstone, wind and sand-eroded at their bases so that they threatened to topple over on the two small specks that followed a tortuous way through their maze. Their spectacular size and shapes were astonishing and caused us to realize our humble insignificance, yet their splotches of shade furnished welcome relief. When not too dazed by its crueler moods, there is a certain beauty and purity in the Arabian wastes, extending in their forbidding isolation as God and time created them and unviolated by human trespass.

We kept a lookout for I hoped we might see a rare oryx if they ventured this far south. I had been anxious to glimpse them in their natural habitat since the year before when Abdul Aziz had presented a pair to Dean Landis at the time I was assigned to his staff in Cairo. I recalled the evening he told me at his home in Zamalek that a pair of oryx had arrived and were at the moment standing in their crates in the back garden. When he added that he did not know what to do with them, I, assuming they were pettable little things, begged him to give them to me. He readily consented with one of his rare smiles and I dashed down to the garden full of excitement to find they were wild, angry animals the size of small donkeys. They were white, with straight saberlike horns fully two feet long which they attempted to thrust through the crate at me. The dean sent them on to the National Zoo in Washington, and today they remain the only oryx in the United States.

The sun increased in intensity and faint gusts of scorching heat blew up the wadi, but we pushed on not even stopping at the small oasis of Sha'ara. Pat, always being as native as possible, wore Arab sandals. He held them on by the grip of his big toe. As so often happened, in bouncing across the rugged watercourse, his sandals became loose and about to fall off just when he had to shift gears or apply the brake quickly. The result was that Pat's feet and sandals became tangled among the brake and gearshift, preventing any action on his part while he concentrated on getting into the sandals again and at the same time trying to keep the flapping headcloth out of his eyes. The car, meanwhile, jolted off in abandon, jumping gulleys and careening around boulders as I grabbed the wheel to avoid them. Pat eventually recovered his sandals and straightened his headropes before returning to the business of getting the car under control. Everything crashed and bounced loose, including my liver and kidneys. The heat and pain of my aching bones and raw back made me short-tempered enough to swear, but Pat remained unperturbed and, dissolving my unspoken anger, began to sing a bawdy Cockney ditty as if such a rocky road were the Champs Elysées.

The afternoon seemed to get hotter and more sultry. A dust spout, yellow and tight looking, appeared far off to our left and as it spun down toward us in a zigzag course, raising dust devils before it, the atmosphere became ominously quiet and motionless. We attempted to outdistance the whirling column but when it changed course so as to intercept us at a distant point, we halted to take cover. When we did, it twisted contrarily and tore down the trail directly toward us, turning in violent eddies and supporting uprooted bushes in its grasp, small pebbles and splinters of glasslike sand and dust. The sun became obscured and the atmosphere assumed a horrible, ochreous light.

Our Arabs, misjudging the storm's distance and speed, had promptly taken advantage of the halt to say their prayers. Ali stood in front leading them through the varied ritual and, while reciting parts alone, then in unison with the other two, kept throwing an appraising glance over his shoulder at the fast approaching *simoom*. Our yelling advice to hurry caused them to increase the tempo of their recitations and gymnastics, until they appeared as figures on a speeding film—rising, kneeling and bowing to jump up again with almost comic agility, while the storm screamed down upon them. They reached the end (I assumed it was the end) and jumped into the truck just as Pat and I threw a blanket quickly over our heads.

In a few moments the loud swish of the *simoom's* passage fell off beyond us and we poked our heads from beneath the blanket like burrowed prairie dogs. Finding the air fairly safe again we started up and continued on, while shaking our heads over the ways of some people.

Late in the evening we reached Duwadami and stopped at the police stand to pass the time of day and accept the hospitality of *gahwa* (coffee). Duwadami was quite large for a desert settlement. Children and dogs ran to the doors of their mud-brick shacks to stare, but the females remained beyond sight.

We quickly pushed onward to avoid camping for the night near any habitations and, when we felt too exhausted to drive longer, camped in a wide rough wadi which felt damp and oppressive from recent rains. Both Hasan and Ali advised there might be snakes about, for they are often plentiful in the desert near water and a rain will bring out horned vipers, cobras and puff-adders as if by magic. Pat and I were too fatigued to give the matter much thought and rested on the running board while the driver, who denied he ever tired, built up a fire and Hasan wandered around to inspect the land. He had not gone far when we heard him threshing among the scrub and on running to him found that he had killed a puff-adder which the butt of his rifle.

It was rather alarming and we wondered after eating if we would not be wise to push on. We knew of desert snakes' strange habits of lying beside one, probably for warmth, either on the blanket or under it, as the fancy took them.

"Oh, I should care," I wearily concluded. "They will probably strike only you, Pat, for I've been given immunity. No snake nor scorpion will ever harm me," I boasted seriously. "I've been given protection by the Snake Goddess!"

"Blimey, 'e's balmy," said Pat, feigning concern.

"Pat," I chided, "don't tell me that in all your travels around the Middle East you've never heard of the Snake Goddess!"

"Never!" he declared. "But nothing would surprise me. What's it all about, chum?"

"Well, I'll tell you," I began, as we both took the precaution of climbing into the command car to talk. "Once when I was in Upper Egypt our *dragoman,* Adam, brought a snakecharmer to me. Adam declared him to be the best in Egypt, of a long line of professional exorcisers. Their principal business was in ridding people's homes and gardens of snakes. Entertaining tourists was but a side-line. Anyway, Adam brought the man to me. His tall, lean body was robed in a black *galabiya* and his head was turbaned in white. There was a strange, abstract air of mysticism about him and I didn't care for his keen, magnetic eyes. He offered to call forth snakes from any place I suggested, including the spot where I sat—the garden of the Winter Palace Hotel.

"He first showed me that no snakes were upon his person and then began to recite from the Book of the Dead and other peculiar invocations while pacing to and fro and sniffing the air like a bird dog. He suddenly halted, and pointing to a nearby stone wall, exclaimed, 'I smell a snake!'

" 'Fine,' I said, 'I hope it's a cobra.'

"He advanced dramatically to the wall and with his cane tapped upon the crumbling rocks. He commanded the snake to come out, repeating his command so vehemently that he soon broke into a sweat. As he pointed to a hole near the ground I was astounded to see the head of a snake appear. At his command it slowly glided sinuously into the sunlight with head raised a foot above ground, its forked tongue moving quickly in and out. It was a viper at least five feet long!

"The charmer knelt down before it and flung out a string of rapid Arabic. The elevated head waved back and forth while the gleaming eyes stared forth hatred. But in a short time it gradually lowered itself, whereupon the charmer reached out and quickly grabbed it behind the head. I stood as fascinated as any tourist while he opened the snake's jaws to show me its fangs. He ran them through a fold of his garment and by gentle pressure toward the back of the jaw forced them to produce drops of venom.

" 'That's really wonderful,' I said quite impressed, 'but I want to see a cobra.'

"The stately ruins of Luxor Temple stood nearby, so I suggested he walk with me there and try his powers for cobra. He consented readily enough but added that he of course could not produce a cobra if one were not there.

"We strolled into a large court of innumerable, tall columns, all of them topped by the unusual lotus-bud capitals. The man at once began a chanting search. In no time at all he stopped in his tracks then strode across the entire court to a spot where a hole existed between two huge granite blocks. As he tapped upon the stone and worked himself into a raging fervor I saw the head of a snake appear in the hole. I backed slowly away to give him plenty of room, but the snake wouldn't come out. When this became evident the snakecharmer rolled up his sleeve and with a speed almost beyond belief, thrust his hand into the hole and yanked out the snake, tossing it quickly beyond him. I plastered myself against the furthermost wall, for it was indeed a cobra, six feet long if an inch!

"It reared angrily and glided swiftly toward its tormentor. He quickly knelt before the serpent's rush, to a level with its wicked head which curved above a full-hooded neck. It stopped several feet before him, the proper distance for a striking leverage. The man's words poured forth so fast even Adam could not understand them, but we did understand his running wet face and intent eyes. It was a battle of will-power between the snake and the man.

"The cobra wavered in the air as if dancing to the chant. It was not dancing, however. It suddenly struck in the motion I make by quickly throwing out my hand from the bent elbow. It moved like lightning, but so did the charmer. In that split second he had thrown forward his own hand to push back the cobra, touching it just below its rounded, pulsing hood. Its hinge for striking was at the point where the elevated body reached the ground. If one were quick enough it could be prevented each time from striking the intended mark by pushing it back before the angle straightened out to any degree. It required swiftness of action unbelievable in a human being. Each time, however, venom splattered on the charmer's *galabiya* and he was careful it shouldn't fly into his eyes.

"The cobra continued to strike in flashes, seeming to increase in anger, and I wondered whose will should prevail, or if the serpent should succeed in moving faster. Neither the charmer's steady black eyes nor the snake's small beady ones ever wavered. His chant never ceased, though sweat poured from his face. Just when it seemed his nerves should fail the giant hood decreased imperceptibly and the furious waving head began to lower as though becoming sleepy. The ritual continued until the snake lay docile but alert on the ground. Its master then extended his hand carelessly to stroke its head and then to pick it up. I heaved a sigh and sat down weakly on a toppled column. The cobra was placed in a round wicker basket along with the viper and covered with a lid.

"I complimented the man and paid him his fee without the usual argument, for I felt he had earned it. As I started to rise he took hold of both my hands and restrained me. He said I was such a fine and generous young man that he wished to give me the Power of the Snake Goddess. I replied with suspicion that I wanted none of his tourist tricks and further fortified my statement with several magic words which every American traveler in Egypt wishes he knew. As they failed to have the usual effect I became interested and listened to his assurances. Without my agreeing, he closed his sharp eyes, still holding my hands, and launched into a long magical incantation. He was indeed a wizard, for I was spellbound and robbed of volition as if mesmerized. When he finally opened them he pronounced me as possessing the charm and informed me that no snake nor scorpion would ever harm me, although I in return must never harm one myself nor divulge this rite to any living person. In time I was able to mutter my thanks, but he detained me, saying that I must now prove his words.

"He removed the lid from the basket and commanded that I pick up a snake. I said I believed him, that it was not necessary to prove it; but he was not satisfied. Seizing my arm, he thrust my hand forward toward the basket where both reptiles lay coiled with raised, hissing heads. I don't know whether I grasped one's neck to prevent its striking me or not, but against my will I did somehow close my hand on one. The sorcerer then withdrew my hand as I held the cobra in fascination. It did not struggle nor impress me with antipathy. He next forced me to pick up the viper, which I did, and as I held one in each hand he draped their long undulating bodies about my neck and arms. I was not repelled by them. I felt no dislike for them although every cell of their cool bodies seemed in motion upon my skin. I did gradually realize myself a hero however, and began to shout for Adam to come and see me. When he joined us he stood admiring the spectacle with a seemingly knowing grin on his face.

" 'All right,' I exclaimed, 'I believe you. Take them off me.'

" 'But first you must promise to give something to the Snake Goddess and to abide by her laws,' my captor replied.

" 'Ah, it is a tourist trick,' I accused him. 'Very well then, only take them and I'll give you whatever you want!'"

"In awed tones he denied my blasphemy and assured me it was all true, as time would prove. When he carefully relieved me of my encumbrances I threw a pound at him and stalked off, not caring if he flung figures at my retreating back in return or not, but nevertheless undecided about the entire incident."

Finishing the tale I glanced at Pat, lazing beside me, to observe its effect. He rewarded me only with the laconic remark, "Pleasant chap, wasn't he?"

We changed the subject to forget snakes, and extinguished the fire to prevent attracting them. When we crawled into our bed rolls Hasan offered the assurance that he would inspect us during the night, if that were any comfort.

The dampness became less noticeable and the overpowering heat of the day gave place to the exquisite freshness of night. The firmament became thickly powdered with stars while a full moon swam in the eastern sky, like a swan in a deep blue lake. I easily forgot the possibility of unpleasant bed companions and fell asleep thinking snatches of Tennyson:

> "Here at least, where nature sickens nothing. Ah,
>   for some retreat
> Deep in yonder shining Orient, where my life began
>   to beat; . . .
> Larger constellations burning, mellow moons and
>   happy skies,
> Breaths of tropic shade and palms in cluster, knots
>   of Paradise. . . .

CHAPTER ELEVEN

Conquering the Summan Dahana

I SLEPT soundly and awoke early, conscious of a near presence in the dark. I realized it to be Hasan as he searched round me with a stick. I lay quietly, holding my breath, until he pronounced me snakeless. At my inquiry as to the Arab method of treatment for snakebite he said that they apply a snakeskin plaster and read or recite chapters of the Koran over the suffering, swelling victim until he died!

"Well, do they ever recover?" I asked.

"*Insha' Allah,*" he carelessly replied.

The wadi where we were camped proved to be the lowest depression between the Hijaz tableland and the Aruma Plateau of the Najd.

During the day we passed many majestic formations of worn granite and old, decaying sandstone, running in long rough, but unbroken ridges and ending in towering buttes with the debris worn loose by the action of centuries lying in riveted flounces at their base. Smooth hard fields of granite and basalt schards made good running until reaching gentle rolls of round yellow sand.

Large, fat lizards, called *dhobs,* dashed in terror for their holes as we roared past spots where they sunbathed. The speed of these ugly monsters was amazing and their propulsion most comical as the short bowed legs pounded the sand and the thick long tail thrashed frantically to and fro. We often raced them with the car but they seemed always capable of producing the necessary speed to reach a hole before we ran them down, their legs moving so fast as to be almost invisible. When we stopped at noontime, Ali dug one out and after bleeding it by Moslem custom, roasted the still thrashing tail over a fire. He insisted it was good and easily persuaded Pat to sample some, but I could not be tempted. Pat claimed it tasted like chicken and the meat, once scraped of its black covering, did at least look like breast of chicken. However, I thought it more to John's taste than mine.

Pat, with enjoyable ceremony, made British army tea, or *shi,* by boiling it until it would have made good dye. Canned milk and sugar was added while it boiled. Although it shriveled my gums and nearly took my teeth out, it was good. While we rested and drank quantities, a caravan of camels loomed on the distant horizon and appeared in the haze like giant birds with ridiculously long legs. When we sped past them an hour later they seemed to be the slowest and most superciliously dignified things that nature could devise.

We lost the truck several times that day and were obliged to retrace our way searching for it. Once we returned ten miles to find it stuck in the sand and another time found that the body had bounced loose and threatened to fall off. We managed by tremendous exertion to right it somewhat and replace one or two u-bolts, hoping it would stay on until we reached Barra where help might be available.

Suddenly we came upon an area of rolling red sand dunes, their crests running from north to south, and realized them to be a spur of the dreaded Summan Dahana. The Dahana is a vicious formation of moving dunes swept down by the winds from the Nafud in the north; pointing like daggers to the heart of Arabia. They sweep around the Aruma Plateau where Riyadh is located and are principally concentrated east of that city, extending all the distance to the Persian Gulf.

The dunes appeared like great ocean waves, smooth on one side and on the other fluted in their entirety into tiny corrugations by the hot winds. Ali warned that we should not attempt to cross this spur, of perhaps twenty miles, except in the early morning when the night dampness held the sands more solid. They looked so formidable it seemed doubtful whether anything could possibly improve them.

However, worn out with fatigue and the heat, we permitted Ali a self-deceiving victory and pulled off to a shallow depression protected by a ridge of wind-break dunes. The sand was smooth and unscarred, for the wind swept the surface like a great soft brush, erasing all traces of former travelers and substituting only in spots a stippled pattern of innumerable tiny virgin waves. The dried camel droppings, which were round and lighter than the sand, escaped over the ripples and formed little piles where the wind had eddied. They were the only indications that other travelers had either rested here before attacking the Dahana or halted after conquering it.

Having to feed three extra mouths was severely taxing our food supplies, but our men confirmed our surmise that no game would be in those parts. Hasan said that not even gazelles inhabited the thirsty area but that leopards, oryx and other game abounded in the disordered steppes farther to the north. I had hoped we might at least get a bustard on the way across. Never once, however, all the while I was in Arabia, did I have the pleasure of feasting on this famous relative of the turkey.

The ill-tempered Ali led his two brothers in prayer while Pat and I sprawled in the sand and the setting sun threw the Dahana into long shadows. Sunlit crests seemed islands of gold interspersed by valleys of darkness, so that a giant could have crossed as on stepping-stones.

As the heat tempered to a pleasant balminess and the desert became breathlessly silent, we heard a distant voice yodeling a Bedouin air. We had thought the nearest oasis to be miles away, and so it was, but in the unobstructed, clear air a voice could carry for unbelievable distances. We heard him again before daybreak, the chant of his mellow notes rolling across the desert, closely pursued by the inflection of clear tenor tones, lilting up and down. The only sound in the half-darkness, its haunting beauty seemed oddly disturbing, like a lost soul wailing in the wilderness.

Before the red sun appeared we were ready to tackle the dunes and Pat obligingly suggested I have the first try. The dunes did not begin in easy stages but by a definite clear line drawn by the magic hand of the wind. We crept up the first incline slowly, careful not to lose traction, all four wheels churning steadily and up to their hubs in the loose fine sand—a veritable sea of tiny bearings, shaped into perfect roundness by their desert passage. As we started down its steep eastern slope the entire surface seemed to shift and the car began to slide sideways until wrestling the wheel turned it to slide the other way. It required every spark of strength and good judgment to maintain a course and keep the car righted so that a speed could be attained, when nearing the bottom, adequate to surmount the next immediate hill. The wheels ground in an angry whirr, spouting four yellow streams of sand which formed into a small trailing sand cloud.

The crests were smooth and more solid, so I stopped where one started down again and found myself streaming in sweat and shaking from fright and exhaustion. When Pat smiled at my state, I warned him, "Don't laugh, buddy, your turn's coming!" He mopped his own brow and said he might prefer walking.

The truck plowed up angrily after us, its big sand tires buzzing like sawmills and on reaching our level bravely rushed to the descent, afraid to stop in the tenacious stuff. It bogged, however, in the next climb and nearly buried itself before we could jump out and reach the spot to end the driver's useless efforts. We warned him he should not again attempt to proceed further once stuck, for it only increased the difficulty of getting free. We shoveled tons of loose sand from around the wheels and as each shovel-full was removed it was at once replaced by the insidious flow of surrounding sand. When the steel tracks were finally in place we had practically a pit from which to climb. Everyone pushed, despite shifting, insecure footing, as the driver gave it the gun and, once rolling, wisely kept going until he reached a distant crest safe enough to halt upon. Poor Ali and Hasan trudged after it like flies in yellow molasses, while we stumbled back to our car with the tracks.

Thus most of the day was spent while the sun beat down on us and its glare inflicted stabbing pains to our eyes. We were always able to extricate ourselves without digging, but the continued failure of the truck began to wear us down until we wondered if we should ever take it through to the end. At one time in our pushing Ali flung himself down on the sand, probably in fatigue and vexation, for he beat the sand with his fists and kicked in a tantrum. So we rested, while teasing him, like a child, back to good humor. At another time though, he bled at the mouth, so we relieved him of further effort and allowed him to ride in the back of our command car, seated atop the baggage in royal importance.

When Pat took over he sensibly removed his sandals and trailing *qhotra* which pleased me, for we could not risk any dangerous tangles in the billows of vicious, sandy sea. To our intense relief we surmounted the last treacherous dune sometime in the afternoon. Then we raced freely over rising plains of good hard surfaced gravel and lava, only bad where the road led down and up through dry chasms. At these points a novice would swear that no machine could possibly climb the tortuous trail and that only a mountain goat might jump the rising, rocky levels. But we made it and the truck with us, its body now held on by rope, wire, sweat and prayer.

We began to question Ali about the remaining distance to Riyadh and each time he replied, "five gallons away," or "around the next mountain," but I still doubted if he knew. We used many "five gallons" and passed around many mountains but Riyadh was never waiting beyond. If I asked Pat's opinion he shrugged in a carefree manner and replied that he "hadn't a clue." I thought, "Ali, and now you!" He seemed so in love with the desert that it didn't matter if we ever reached Riyadh. His happiness poured out in an endless repertoire of bawdy English songs.

The only milestones so far had been an occasional pile of scattered, bleached bones where a camel had foundered and had probably been eaten on the spot by its owners who left the remains for vultures to gorge on.

Limestone ribs became exposed on the Najd slopes and where the plain could be viewed on a level it appeared green in spots with wiry grass that was not visible when viewed from above. The shifting mirage disguised height and distance so that flocks of goats on the horizon were taken to be camels and surprised us when they turned out to be merely goats. We reserved judgment when a herd appeared in the late afternoon and did not pronounce them camels until right upon them. Their keeper had run ahead at our approach to intercept us, extending a tin container before him in his crazy flight. Since he reached our passing point before us, we stopped and agreed to give him water if he would give us milk. The herd belonged to the king and were out at pasture, some of them with foals. The Bedou accepted a cooking pan and approached the nearest milch-camel. While he milked it full she stood patiently but loudly lamenting her fate to high heaven.

The camels seen in Arabia are the single-humped dromedaries. The two-humped bactrians are only found in Iran, Turkestan and Mongolia and are shaggy, ponderous beasts raised only for their soft, luxurious wool and for pack animals.

No creature possesses more disagreeable characteristics and none present such a strange enigma. The camel will go for days without food or water and then subsist on only sticks and sharp thorns. He will plod for fantastic distances, carrying incredible loads through terrific heat and burning sand which would kill a less enduring creature. But when his reserves of water and energy do finally become exhausted he reaches a sudden end of endurance and collapses in dramatic protest, perhaps never to rise again.

No creature is more treacherous or more evil tempered. There is no room in his staunch heart for affection toward anyone. Though his looks pretend indifference, he is constantly alert for possibilities to throw his load or to bite the man who feeds and cares for him. If ever done an injury he is revengeful enough to carry the grudge for years until finding the chance to kill his offender. From birth until death the camel vociferously accuses his owner and the world in general, constantly complaining and groaning as if he were the most abused and ill-treated of all God's creatures. I believe, however, this is not without some justification, although he does overdo it.

It is not unusual for a camel, when spoken to or prodded forward to turn his ugly head completely around on the long, serpent-like neck and glare hatefully from beneath long, lowered eyelashes directly into the face of the man on his back. This action alone is disconcerting enough, but the disagreeable beast promptly follows his withering look with an evil-smelling, humid bawl which nearly unseats his rider.

We sat on the running-board, drinking our milk and contemplating the grazing herd before us.

"What an extraordinary animal he is," Pat thoughtfully observed. "He is so contrary to nature—why even his most important appendage is a freak. Just look; it's put on backward!"

We laughed at the haughty, arrogant beasts, for this indeed appears to be true. It is not only exceedingly small for such a large animal but instead of extending forward, as with other normal creatures, the male genital organ grows between the animal's legs and points to the rear.

The Arabs have a thousand stories to tell concerning their "greatest gift from God." Without the camel the Bedouin would be unable to live. Some say it is this knowledge of his importance which accounts for the camel's pretentious, imperious air. Others say it is because only he knows the one hundredth name for God which gives him his smug demeanor. All these stories are entertaining and may be logical, but the Arab's reason for the camel's querulous disposition are more amusing to me.

The most colorful story and the one most frequently told all over the Arab world with variations, has for its setting the time of the flood, a catastrophe vividly recent to the Arabs.

They tell how Noah built the Ark and when the rains began he informed the animals that only one pair of each kind would be permitted to enter. It occurred to his practical wife that should all these animals begin to breed and to have young while weathering the long deluge, the Ark would soon be dangerously overcrowded. Noah admitted such a possibility was, indeed, a matter for serious consideration and would certainly require stern measures of control.

After much careful study it was again his wife who proposed the only positive prevention against such goings-on would be to have each male passenger check a particular part of his person at the gate on entering the Ark. The understanding Noah conceded it was the only practical answer to the problem.

When the passengers were informed of the shipboard rules there was little objection, except possibly on the part of some of the lesser but more active members. The animals as a whole, however, realized the seriousness of the situation and agreed to such temporary inconvenience.

As they crowded into the Ark each checked his valuable property with Mrs. Noah who carefully locked them in a closet. She is supposed to have numbered them but in the rush neglected to give to each any means of identification, never guessing what might be the awful consequence of her inexperience.

All went well on the voyage. Eventually the rains ceased, then the wind blew and blew until dry land appeared and the Ark settled upon the top of Mount Ararat.

The passengers were naturally most anxious to disembark after the long voyage. However, their landing was handled again by Mrs. Noah, who seems to have attended to all details, with proper order and despatch. Everything went smoothly, without confusion or incident, each male creature reclaiming his personal valuables as he filed out the door. That is, until the very end.

Everyone knows it is a toss-up between the camel and the donkey as to which is the most indolent. In this case the donkey came at the end of the line, with Mr. Camel just before him. His anxious mate finally became annoyed with the slow-moving camel ahead and urged her husband forward. He slipped past the complacent camel and reached for his property. It may have been the excitement which caused Mrs. Noah to make her first serious mistake. But whatever it was, she seems to have instinctively reached for the most prominent of the only two articles remaining on the shelf. The sensible donkey grabbed it and wisely made off, followed by his wife, without comment or even an expression of thanks.

The ambling camel next approached Mrs. Noah as she reached for the last small thing left in her care. She started to hand it over but on seeing the object proffered him, Mr. Camel looked aghast. He disdainfully declared there must be some mistake, for that insignificant thing was certainly not his! Furthermore, he was highly insulted at the very inference in the matter.

The uncertain Mrs. Noah said no, she did not think any mistake had been made; the last of the animals had gone and this was all that remained. However, she would look further. She searched about without success and turning to Mr. Camel insisted it must be his.

Well, as the argument advanced Mr. Camel surpassed himself in indignation. He declared that such a trifle could not be foisted upon him. He only wanted what was his own or else nothing at all! Up to this point he had had the full support of his wife, but she now became disturbed with this turn of affairs. She, as well as Mrs. Noah, grew most alarmed when her husband finally announced that he preferred going without until such time as Mrs. Noah in some way rectified the mistake she had obviously made. With this ultimatum he gathered his pride and stalked from the Ark, leaving his wife and Mrs. Noah gaping in bewilderment.

Mrs. Noah soon realized what a tragedy this could be. It would undoubtedly mean the extinction of one of God's most valuable creatures. Visualizing the serious consequence of her error, as well as the retreating back of Mr. Camel, she became frantic and quickly determined to take some action which might absolve her own responsibility in the mishap. On the theory that at least something was better than nothing, she impulsively seized the rejected object and dashed down the gangplank.

The legend does not relate where Mr. Noah was all the while, but in his wife's defense it must be said that, although she had handled the delicate task of checkroom mistress, this by no means qualified her as an anatomist.

On overtaking Mr. Camel she quickly and with great determination thrust forward the spurned appendage and stuck it firmly beneath his indignant tail. In her hurry and agitation she committed a second offense. She placed it on backward!

So the Arabs say that to this day the little donkey contentedly carries an appendage quite out of proportion to his size and the lumbering camel appears destined to go on through time justly protesting his own sad misfortune; all of which is a superb tribute to the Arab imagination and sense of humor.

CHAPTER TWELVE

The Court of His Majesty Abdul Aziz

THE milk was good and refreshing and tasted like rich, warm cow's milk. We left the herder with many *salaams* and a container of water, which was all we had left to offer.

Each time we spied a distant Bedou tending his few goats or camels, he invariably tucked up his robes and started in a wild, comical dash to waylay us. It was impossible to give more than a cupful to all who beseeched us, and we wondered what they did for water if no one passed by to relieve them. It was sometimes cruel fun to outrace them but we always felt sorry and guilty when they dejectedly gave up, despairing of reaching us.

The Najd Desert, a plateau of some three-thousand feet elevation, assumed great dome-shaped, rolling formations, packed solid with a mixture of gravel, lava and little sand, permitting the best speed of the trip. As flocks became more numerous, as did carcasses from which rose flapping, ugly vultures with long white necks and bald red heads, it was apparent that a community could not be far off. When we stopped for prayers Ali suggested we camp, and since he seemed reasonably certain this time that Riyadh was actually over the next rise, we agreed.

Next morning he advised us to shave, since we had been unable to grow respectable Arab beards, and to wash all over. This required little encouragement for we now felt able to spare the water. Pat shaved off his week's growth with great reluctance but I was happy to be rid of mine. Then Ali told us to dress in our Arab robes, which we did, trusting that he at last knew what he was doing. I had dressed lightly, failing to bring anything to wear under my *thob,* and felt quite naked and exposed in the filmy robes. After Pat promised to see that I did not stand between an audience and the sunlight, we assembled our gowns like old women entering a carriage, and settled in the car for a hoped-for grand entry into the capital.

Breasting the first rise, we halted to view the city, gathered together on the distant plain by an imposing battlemented stone and earthen wall, above which waved the welcoming green banners of innumerable palm fronds.

The great wonder of Riyadh is that one comes upon it so suddenly. It is so hidden in the wilderness of shapeless, calcareous undulations that when it bursts into view one simply stops to gaze in wonder, repeating unbelievingly, "Riyadh! Riyadh!" It is so impressively a fitting retreat for such a desert monarch as His Majesty, Abdul Aziz;

a fact that is accentuated by the endless pain of reaching it.

Rounded, slightly conic defense towers appeared at intervals, rising above their broad bases on the high, mud-plastered brick wall; pierced by occasional structural beams and gun slots and topped by decorative serrations. Rising beyond the wall could be seen the delicate spires of white minarets, girthed by two or three *muezzin* balconies which decreased in size with their elevation.

The Thumairi Gate, two large, square, white-plastered holes in the wall, was overbuilt by a square tower, similarly pierced by short extensions of round wooden beams and corniced with small, pyramidal-stepped formations of plaster.

Ali, still riding on the back seat, directed us to turn sharply before reaching the police-guarded city gate and, crossing a wide, dust-laden square, we halted instead at a similar gate, the entrance to a tremendous, rambling structure just outside the city. Its own wide, brown walls were turreted, plainly pargetted and topped by an escalloped cornice. We realized it to be the Maruba Palace of Crown Prince Saud, Viceroy of the Najd, and assumed we would merely pay our courtesies to him as is customary.

At a word from Ali one of the guards disappeared at a trot, holding his rifle close to his side. He soon reappeared followed by the puffing captain of the guard who salaamed and begged us to follow him at once. He led the way through a vast courtyard, parked with many royal limousines and through another imposing, arcaded gateway to an inner court. A wide cement promenade was lined on both sides by black, stalwart looking royal Najdean guards, brilliantly accoutered in handsome robes and beautiful but fierce looking gold and silver-sheathed weapons. We endeavored to saunter between their attentioned ranks with almost a bored air of nonchalance, gathering our robes about us in both hands while gripping our sandals in precaution with each big toe; wanting to giggle and feeling "on-stage" for the first time.

The captain led the way through still another white colonnaded court and delivered us into the hands of the palace chamberlain. He in turn escorted us up a broad tiled stairway, past mosaic halls and into a large, heavily carpeted anteroom where stood knots of whispering, official-looking Arabs in flashing costumes.

The chamberlain, as if we were expected, bade us enter the adjoining audience chamber. Before passing through the portal, we added our sandals to the great array already assembled there. Pat, suddenly timid, shoved me ahead, so that I rather burst into the long narrow room as if tossed there. Collecting myself I proceeded barefoot and weak-kneed, followed by Pat, I hoped, between two long lines of standing audience. The substantial figure seated at the far end rose from his high gilt chair, greatly surprising me. It was *not* the Emir Saud!

I paced steadily toward him, however, until close enough to salaam, while touching my forehead and heart. I then took the massive outstretched hand of none other than His smiling Majesty, Abdul Aziz, Prince of the Faithful and Lord of Arabia.

The king motioned us to be seated, one on either side in gilt chairs similar to his own. I was no sooner seated than I quickly jumped up, blatantly shattering the silence with an exclamation, for standing in the audience before the king was an American friend, also in Arab costume. The king slapped his leg and laughed for he grasped the significance of the incident at once. Turning to my friend, he said in Arabic, "There! you make such a good Arab even your own people cannot recognize you!" He laughed heartily while I remained speechless, wondering how Clark could be standing before us when we had left him in Jidda.

The king continued to beam in amusement as Clark informed us that he had flown over in His Majesty's plane only that morning, along with several of the Royal cabinet, including Sheikh Abdullah.

The king's coffee-slave stepped forward just then with a beaked brass pot in one hand and a stack of fragile looking egg-shell cups clinking in the other. With an accomplished flourish, perfected through years of practice, he dashed a few drops of bitter cardamom tea to the uppermost cup, extended some distance away, and proffered it with another efficient gesture. While we sipped them carefully to enjoy the last bitter drop, he stood nearby until they were empty. He then stretched his hand to clap them noisily one above the other and to toss out another cup with a lesser flourish. In returning the second one I remembered to jiggle it slightly to indicate a sufficiency while quickly uncrossing my legs, realizing that the bottoms of my feet were rudely showing.

Sheikh Yusuf Yasin, the deputy foreign minister, sat at his sovereign's feet acting as interpreter. I politely inquired about the king's health and that of his sons, to which His Majesty replied with an eloquent, *"Al hamdu l'illah!"* which implied that all were well, praise God, and to which we immediately added our own, *"Al hamdu l'illah!"*

The king was greatly pleased about our trip to Al Kharj and made several inquiries relative our interest and help in his pet agricultural project. As the conversation became general I relaxed to study him.

The checkered red-and-white headcloth and simple camelwool robes did not set His Majesty apart, yet without pose or effort he dominated the assembly, impressing me with the fact that he was not only keenly aware of everything in his audience chamber but also all the complexity of events in the outside world as well. He seemed an exceptionally large man, every inch of his six-foot-four being truly majestic. His face, although rugged, with an enveloping black beard and mustache, appeared the most benevolent and spiritually illumined I had yet been privileged to behold. I had long admired the staggering accomplishments of this greatest of Arab monarchs, but to realize his presence was even more inspiring. I felt awed by the conviction that here was a man divinely inspired. Although we were unable to converse directly, his personality radiated beyond the speech barrier and I would have sensed his graciousness and spiritual force had he remained silent.

After some time Sheikh Yusuf arose from his position on the floor saying that the king had only entered Riyadh for the occasion of granting audience and must return to his desert camp. The ministers and privy council filed past to shake our hands and we then requested His Majesty's permission to retire. When this was granted with a nod of his head, we again shook his powerful hand, salaamed and withdrew, accompanied by the amiable minister, Sheikh Abdullah.

Sheikh Abdullah escorted us through a labyrinth of passages to our guest quarters and left us with the promise that he would be available for audience after we rested.

Our shaded, cool quarters, with their high-beamed ceilings, were soothing relief from the agony and chaos of the desert. We tore off our *qhotras* and reclined on the splendor of thick Oriental rugs, among the mass of pillows which lined all walls; spurning the two brass beds for their only intruding note in the room. Such was our Spartan but Eastern luxury and we reveled in it.

A slave soon brought in iced drinks, followed shortly by others pushing wheeled tables bounteously laden with all manner of Arab dishes covered with silver lids. Most were goat or lamb in one form or another, dripping with *ghee* and other sauces; a delicious change from our desert fare.

After finishing the meal with a bowl of *laban* (curdled camel's milk), a servant brought basins of rose-scented water so we might bathe. Then, donning our *qhotras,* we strolled about the outside balcony, a wide shaded veranda running around the four sides of the tiled, central courtyard. The supporting pillars were pedestaled white plaster and the solid plaster railing was topped by decorations of the same material formed into odd shapes, as one would obtain by cutting a string of dolls from folded paper.

The mosaic-covered walls were broken at regular intervals by doors leading into other chambers and as we passed one we noticed four young Air Force officers within. Pat commented that they must be the American crew assigned to fly the king's plane, a C-47 just presented to him by President Roosevelt. Excitedly I suggested we make their acquaintance. So we returned to tap on their open door and to step in, while greeting them in Arabic. All four of them jumped to their feet and stood stiffly before us.

"That's all right fellows," I said, laughing. "Sit down—I'm an American too."

But they did not believe me and continued to look rather shy, taking us to be several of the English-speaking royal family. We then pulled off our headcloths and introduced ourselves and finally they all began to laugh.

"Well I'll be damned," they exclaimed. "What the hell are you guys doing out in *this* place?" We explained and found them to be as surprised at our strange fate as we had been at theirs.

When Pat and I returned to our room the king's chamberlain appeared bearing royal gifts; a gold watch for each of us inscribed with the king's name, handsome *mishlahs,* cashmere headcloths and royal *agals.* An Arab tailor also stood ready to fit the robes to our measurements. The chamberlain delivered an invitation from His Majesty to attend an Arab feast at his desert camp that afternoon. When leaving he kindly carried a message for us requesting an audience with Sheikh Abdullah.

When later received by the sheikh, we learned that the king had ordered that his plane should take us on to Dhahran on the Persian Gulf, after our visit to Al Kharj, if that was agreeable to us. It was indeed, so we arranged all plans, then checked with our new friends, the crew, to make certain they understood we would be picked up on the desert beyond the prohibited area two days later at a given hour.

Sheikh Abdullah and his party escorted us that afternoon to the royal camp which was located out on the desert more than an hour's drive from the city. His Majesty spends most of his time between his desert camp and the Badia Palace of Crown Prince Saud, in the paradisiacal setting of Wadi Badin.

We were driven to a spot not far from the king's tent where, spread on the desert sand, were many rugs on which were placed rows of overstuffed furniture, sofas and gilded chairs. They created a very odd appearance in the open desert. His Majesty was sitting there surrounded by a large party. At least fifteen of his forty-odd sons were present and one small daughter, in whom he seemed to take fond delight.

The sons were all tall and slim, some very light complexioned and others darker, because most of them had different mothers. Most were aquiline featured and bore a marked patrician look. They all had uncommonly long, slim and well-formed hands and fingers. Although several of the young teen-age princes whom I had met on the Red Sea coast had seemed rather arrogant and imperious, today in the presence of their father they were all on their most proper and gently-bred behavior.

We learned that the king wished us the pleasure of seeing his famous herds of pedigreed camels. We were no sooner seated than they started past in droves, driven by their herdsmen. Many of them were large, handsome white beasts, found nowhere but in the Najd and trained for riding and racing. The Saudi herds have been famed for many years as the finest blooded and riding beasts of the Middle East.

As one she-camel passed nearby with a young foal beside her, the small princess leaning on her father's knee clapped her hands in admiration and glee. The king smiled and, while petting the child, promised that if she liked it, it should be hers.

The droves were followed by mounted camel-cavalry, the characteristic soldiers of the Najd who are known as *Hajjians* or dromedarists. As they passed in trotting formations each held his rifle aloft while shouting loud war cries. An exciting exhibition of racing camels came next, the riders perched atop the high saddles while their mounts ran in a grotesque manner with long necks stretched straight before them. They were capable of unsuspected speed and seemed to support the claim that camels can run faster than horses, although I never saw an Arabian horse anywhere in Arabia. It is too hot for them in the southern parts of the country, but they are bred in the Najd and very extensively in the north.

Small camel units passed in the rising dust, demonstrating the various Arab paces; the finest seeming to be a bent-kneed gait with much swinging of the fetlock, the stride appearing longer and quicker than the normal and the body seeming to move smoother. The quick marching gait, of about twelve miles per hour, seemed to be a somewhat fast pace in which both legs on one side moved forward simultaneously. The king beamed broadly if not proudly, during the show, his brow clouding whenever his frequent smile faded away.

One of the princes had approached my chair and, being able to speak English and wishing to be friendly, he explained that Arabs of means ride none but she-camels since they move more smoothly under the saddle than males, are better tempered and less noisy. He claimed they are also more patient and will endure to march long after they are worn out, indeed, until they totter with exhaustion and fall in their tracks to die. The coarser males will grow angry, fling themselves down when overly tired and from sheer rage or spite die there unnecessarily. In fact, it is claimed that they do actually die sometimes for no other reason than rebellious spite.

After the demonstration the usual ceremonial coffee and tea was served, then we were bidden to enter the dining tent, its sand floor covered by many layers of carpets. Dinners in the palace for Western visitors are always served European style, with the finest silver, china and gold service, but feasts on the desert are always Arab style and to dine with the king in that manner is considered a rare honor.

As we entered the tent two servants staggered in carrying a large tinned copper tray between them, followed by a number more. The trays were all placed on the carpets down the center of the tent. Florid Arabic characters were incised round the trays. Someone translated one to me reading, "To the glory of Allah and in trust of His mercy —property of His poor supplicant, Abdul Aziz Ibn Abdur-Rahman Al Faisal Al Saud."

Each tray was five feet across and piled high with a mountain of white rice, its top formed into a large crater where lay several carcasses of barbecued sheep. The heads, livers and other parts had been boiled separately and the heads then placed on the edge of the crater, propped on their severed stumps. A servant ladled from a copper kettle small succulent morsels of meat, the livers and blobs of tail-fat, all swimming in the *ghee* and juice from their cooking. The gravy was ladled out until the large tray became brimming and its hot savory odor filled the tent.

The king waved his hand for all to be seated, but everyone seemed blind and deaf, as good manners demanded, until gradually one by one they stepped forward to sink down upon one knee round a tray. Each tray accommodated fifteen or more people and we, sticking close to Sheikh Abdullah, edged round one, rolled back our right sleeve to the elbow and, taking our cue from him, murmured, "In the name of Allah . . ." dipping into the hot dripping rice, being careful not to burn our fingers in the liquid fat.

As His Majesty is arthritic and cannot kneel, he was seated in a comfortable large chair at one end of the tent where, being a light eater, he was served small amounts of titbits and choice morsels. I had occasion to note the truth of Philby's words:

"The Prophet was always partial to three indulgences: women, scents and food. He had experience and to spare of the first two with but slender opportunity for the last. The present wearer of the Prophet's mantle in Arabia admits to full experience and knowledge of women and sweet perfumes, but to food and sleep he is a stranger. His frugality in the former is the terror of his guests who have to eat avidly to rise contentedly when he quits his table."

Pat and I could knead between our fingers small balls of rice stuck together by bits of meat and sufficient pressure, but afraid to project them into our mouths Arab fashion by leverage of the thumb and crooked forefinger, we played safe by dropping the delicious pellets into our mouths after tilting back our heads. It required practice, however, to obtain the right construction so the little lumps would hold together and yet come free from the fingers, not falling to pieces and spilling over us. The fingers had to be licked clean to prevent any cooling grease holding the next morsel when it should fall into the mouth.

As the meat pile cooled one reached over to tear bits off here and there. No eye was offered either of us, as so many strangers expect, although I knew it would not have disturbed Pat. However, Sheikh Abdullah did tear out a tongue and plop a choice share of it on the tray before me. I only smiled my thanks, as is proper, and ate it with relish. More hearty souls pulled great hunks from the carcasses, using their dagger or whole hand, but no one at that feast cracked open a skull for the enclosed *pièce de résistance*.

Cavities were eaten into the pile of rice and the carcasses dwindled as each diner slowed down, picking half-heartedly here and there and finally ceasing altogether. Before the last seemed satisfied, however, everyone rose as at a signal for it was noticed the king had finished. Each guest murmured loud praises and blessings on him and retired to the side of the tent where stood slaves with bowls of scented water, towels and very necessary soap.

Rather than sit on chairs, which were ranged to one side, we sat upon the carpet with feet folded under, as did everyone else. A young slave walked about wafting frankincense from a brazier, and, while the trays were removed beyond sight for feasting the king's retinue, coffee was served until each courteously refused the fourth cup.

I had observed during the course of the afternoon that the king appeared to be almost debonair in manner. Although to me he seemed optimistic, confident and democratic, it is said that now in his ripening years he is inclined to be despotic at times and laconic in speech; except in conversation with one of his old friends when the topic turns to women, war or past adventures.

Abdul Aziz is a born ruler and knows his religion and his people as no other man could. They have been his life's study. His closest mentor, St. John Philby, concedes, however, that he is a supreme master of his craft when dealing with internal affairs of Arabia and disappointing only when he leaves the well-known paths for the strange fields of finance and economics.

There is actually no such person as Ibn Saud. This name is a mistake and made so often in the press that it has come into common usage outside Arabia. There is only one King of Saudi Arabia and he is Abdul Aziz Ibn Abdur-Rahman Al Faisal Al Saud. He is referred to and signs himself Abdul Aziz, or occasionally and slightly more formally, Abdul Aziz Al Saud. The "Al Saud" means "of the family of Saud." The "Ibn Abdur-Rahman" merely signifies "the son of Abdur-Rahman." Saud is his family name and Faisal is also a family name.

The Sauds ruled the Najd for many generations and, even though during the time of Abdul Aziz' father quite a large area was for awhile under their control, the family had fallen so that by the time Abdul Aziz was ten years old he was an exile in Kuwait—a tiny sheikhdom at the head of the Persian Gulf. The family naturally wished to regain power in their own territory and Abdul Aziz' entire life has been dedicated to building a united Arabia. He first regained Riyadh then all of the Najd by a series of daring exploits with only a handful of followers. He went on to gradually subdue the tribes in an ever increasing territory in all directions.

The final step was the conquering of the Kingdom of the Hijaz, on the Red Sea. Mecca surrendered in time, without resistance, and Abdul Aziz entered the city for the first time in his life on December 5, 1924, in all humility and dressed in the garb of a pilgrim. King Hussein had abdicated under the protection of a British warship. He eventually moved to Cyprus and spent the last years of his life there. The British, however, set up his family, the Hashimite house, as rulers of the newly formed state of Transjordan. Meanwhile one of his sons, Ali, proclaimed himself king and held out in the walled city of Jidda. Abdul Aziz laid seige to the city but did not attack, except for a desultory bombardment. By the fall of 1925 thousands of people had died of thirst, hunger and disease. Medina surrendered to Abdul Aziz' third son, Mohammed, and shortly after Jidda surrendered also, leaving Abdul Aziz as the undisputed Lord of all Arabia. It was not until January 8, 1926, however, that he was informed of the decision of the people to proclaim him as King of the Hijaz; an honor which he accepted humbly and without ceremony, in keeping with the simplicity of his religious faith.

Sheikh Abdullah had approached the king to sit conversing at his feet, but when we saw him rise to depart, we too approached to express our appreciation and take leave.

Shaking hands once again, His Majesty murmured *"Allah Yibarak fik"* ("God bless you") and we quietly withdrew to return by motor to our quarters in Riyadh.

CHAPTER THIRTEEN

The Oasis of Al Kharj

AFTER breakfast the next morning, we left the palace for the trip to Al Kharj and found our command car where we had left it near the palace gate. Our escort were waiting in the truck as if they had been sitting there the entire time.

We drove slowly through Riyadh, the city which many historians claim comes close to being the world's capitol city of religious and racial pride. It is located in the Wadi Hanifa and is 1,700 feet above sea level. It appeared as a sprawling desert city of grays and browns, built of sun-dried mud brick and carpeted in layers of dry, gray dust. There seemed to be an amazing amount of activity, the lanes animated with robed figures, camel caravans and surprising numbers of vehicles. There was a noticeable absence of cats and dogs, so abundant in other Arabian cities. Open pools of running water appeared in depressions, edged by countless date palms which shaded the watering flocks, giving the town a rural air.

Just south of the crenelated walls of Riyadh we passed the king's own palace, an immense, extensive structure of brown, sun-dried clay, quite plain except for its top edging of huge frills, stepped up to their central peaks that assumed the shape of phallic symbols. Ali said that ramps lead to various levels of the palace, facilitating the king's easy passage from one floor to another, and that an elevator had just been installed for his private use. The harem was a separate large building, connected to the main palace by colonnaded corridors that skirted a vast central garden or courtyard.

It is said that well over five thousand persons compose the royal household, a vast clan to be sure, and that more than six hundred vehicles crowd the palace garage. Many of the sons are married and they too have their harems and countless children. It is easy to understand how the matrimonial affairs of the Wahhabi royal family are so extremely complex.

When Abdul Aziz was still only a boy, he married a little Bedouin girl. She died six months later and his next wife was Jauhara, the love and inspiration of his life. He never divorced her and in fact made her his queen. When she died in 1918 during the influenza plague, as did their beloved first-born, Turki, it all but broke his stout heart. Since then it has been the king's custom to keep three wives with the fourth place empty so that he may marry whenever he finds it desirable or expedient. Should there be no vacant place when he needs one, he divorces a wife to make the necessary vacancy. Even had time permitted, Abdul Aziz would never have kept concubines or had forbidden liaisons and illegitimate children, for he lives strictly and devoutly by the rules laid down by the Prophet.

Christ gave no instructions to Christians regarding marriage but Mohammed claimed to complete the revelations of Christ by saying, "Thou mayest take two, three or four wives, but no more." Mohammed placed wives in a high position with special property rights. He specified alimony in case of divorce and declared that they should be treated well, saying further, "If thou canst not deal equally and justly with each and all, thou shalt take only one." But he also made divorce an easy matter. Should a man wish to divorce a wife it is only necessary for him to repeat, "I divorce thee," three times in front of witnesses. However, although the woman is cast off, she must be provided for.

During his life Ibn Saud has enjoyed women as wives and companions and mothers of his children. As he observes the principles of his religion he makes no explanations nor apologies for his numerous marriages. He has broken no conventions and needs no excuses. It is reported that some years ago, while discussing marriage and divorce with his friend and confidant, Philby, the king declared, "I follow the Prophet—the peace of God be upon him. What he sends I take and what he enjoins I obey. My wives shall always be the number that he has allowed. I have married and divorced a hundred wives and if God wills, I shall marry and divorce many more."

On another occasion Philby quotes the king as saying, "By Allah! In my lifetime I have indeed married many women and by the grace of God I have not done with wiving yet! I am still young and strong. Now with the losses of the war, assuredly the time will come when the people of Europe will see wisdom and the men take more wives than one each!"

The king cannot understand a man having only one wife. He considers it unnatural and a subject for jest. But for a man to have none at all he regards as a sin before God. His Majesty derives the greatest pleasure in promising to provide wives for several Americans with whom he has become well acquainted. It is done in a robust sense of humor but in a serious vein, for he enjoys their discomfort, especially if they already have a wife in the United States. He pities the man with only one wife and when discussing such an unfortunate man he pounds the floor with his cane, shouting, "By Allah! They should go to the doctors and be revived!"

The king has married for many reasons. Sometimes he has married for political reasons so as to strengthen his position by alliances with important families. Often it has been to cement the loyalty of a newly conquered tribe or to raise up a family that has fallen on evil days. Sometimes it is from a sense of duty, as when he married the widow of his dead brother, Sa'd. But more often it is because being a vigorous, healthy man he desires women and enjoys their company. It is still said that the king loves a good fight and a good scent, and that he is an accomplished lover.

Abdul Aziz has married one by one into all the landed families and has had wives from the Sudair tribe, the Hijaz, Ataiba, Ajman, Mutair, Anaza and Dawasir tribes. If these wives bore children there was a direct bond of blood. If they remained childless and were divorced he settled money on them and the matter produced no stigma. Many of his ex-wives were married off to various other tribal chiefs, sheikhs or amirs. Such men considered it fortunate and a great honor to possess a woman who had once been the wife of their sovereign. This custom has proved an incalculable force in welding the country into a tightly knit nation by closely associating the various leading families and tribes with the royal family itself. Those divorced women for whom the king found no new husbands lived on in the harem, well cared for, and those who were mothers were given slaves, houses and money with which to bring up the children.

The king is credited for having always treated his women well, married or divorced. He enjoys the company and companionship of his wives and children and it has been his life's habit to go for awhile to his harem after evening prayer and at the completion of the day's work. The king is now in his late seventies but it is said to this day that no wife has ever complained that he neglected her.

Many of the king's sons have responsible positions in the administration of the country. His Royal Highness Prince Saud, the Crown Prince, is Viceroy of the Najd and His Majesty's chief aide. He administers the affairs of the state when the king is absent from Riyadh. His wisdom, ability and humble manner have won him great respect abroad and a firm place in the hearts of his countrymen. The second son, His Royal Highness Prince Faisal, is Viceroy of the Hijaz, Minister of Foreign Affairs and chief of the Saudi Arabian delegation to the United Nations. He is more familiar to the outside world than any of the other princes and in his special capacities renders outstanding service to his country. His Royal Highness Prince Mansur was minister of defense up until the time of his recent death. Emir Abdulla, the king's brother, is his closest adviser.

The number of daughters by the king is not known and Moslem custom forbids their being introduced to visitors. It is not polite to inquire about the female members of an Arab family and doing so would be considered most offensive.

Leaving the palace behind and forgetting the interest of its household, we proceeded toward Al Kharj. The trail led over the rolling Najd of hard flint and gravel and was edged on the east by continuous saffron-colored escarpments. These were part of the long chain of the Tuwaiq Mountains. The area was more populated than any area we had yet passed but still desert, sparsely covered with tufts of yellow grass and wild lavender where I had expected to see some green pastureland. Small oases were more frequent and livestock more plentiful and stronger looking, as were the Najdean.

As we bumped along the corrugated trail our thoughts returned to the king and his court and Pat recalled an amusing story he had heard about one of the king's ministers. The minister in question had risen to his high position not only through the loyalty of the king to his old friends, but also through his own extreme aggressiveness and ambition. He was fond of holding the center of the stage on all possible occasions and could be depended upon to steal every scene of which he was a part. When pictures were taken of the king and his council, he always emerged conspicuously and, even if in the background, his face would be thrust forward between others or would peer around the shoulder of the king. His Semitic features, black side-whiskers and beard only added to his comical appearance, as though he were only a Hollywood caricature of an Arabian sheikh. As a result he was regarded as something of a court clown.

"Not long ago," Pat went on with his story, "the king was holding a conference with some of the oil men. A large map was spread on the floor before the king's chair and at one point in the discussion they experienced some difficulty in finding a certain location. The king knew where it was and tried to point it out with his walking cane, but his "court clown" seized the opportunity to display his own knowledge of Arabia. He jumped forward, bent down to his knees and, while searching for the spot, turned his back on the king. Being within easy reach, the king quietly placed one huge foot squarely upon the offender's elevated rear and gave a mighty shove. A very surprised minister landed in a heap before the startled guests. The king roared with laughter and after pointing the spot out with his cane, continued the discussion in a jolly and refreshed mood while his clown gathered up what dignity he could find from the map of Arabia."

We laughed at the picture as we sped along. It reminded me of another story about the king's sense of humor as told me by Colonel Eddy. He had been discussing Arab philosophy with the king, the great abuse of the expression, *"insha' Allah"* and the Arab's habit of qualifying every statement, regardless how trivial, by adding, "if God wills." Their conversation then turned to the matter of a large refrigerator which Colonel Eddy had presented the king for his Riyadh palace. Colonel Eddy inquired how the king liked it and His Majesty assured him it was a truly marvelous invention—although there was one curious objection. It seemed that the water jugs always burst after standing in the refrigerator for awhile. The minister was surprised at this but said that the cause was very simple. He explained to the king that the mechanism, being turned up too high, caused the water to freeze and that in freezing it expanded. Since the space was limited, the forming ice naturally burst the vessel in its expansion. Ice was doubtless a new experience for the king, but he nodded his head and allowed that Colonel Eddy's explanation could be the proper scientific one. Then he repeated his words thoughtfully, adding that one unforgettable phrase with a twinkle in his eye, "Yes, that *could* happen —*insha' Allah!*"

Our agricultural mission of eight men were delighted to see us when we reached Al Kharj and happy to learn that someone had remembered them. Their first few months spent in that distant spot, when communications and supplies were not reaching them, caused the men to feel that they had been transported from their Arizona farms to the wasteland of Arabia only to be forgotten. I promised to do what I could by going on to Cairo and reporting their plight in person, promising that cables would fly between there and Washington.

They did have their disheartening difficulties, to be sure, and were at that time completely dependent on the bounty of the king and the oil company. Agricultural machinery and seeds, ordered before they left the United States, were late in arriving and they were even without transportation of any kind. When the equipment did begin to arrive, much of it was found to be damaged by the sea water in its trip half-way round the world. Their first crops had been consumed by hoards of locusts just when ready to harvest and the rows of young trees stripped bare.

Despite such numerous handicaps they had already succeeded in launching a long-range project of reclaiming the fertile desert soil. Three thousand acres were under irrigation at the time, watered by four diesel engines connected to four deep-well turbine pumps that had previously been installed by Aramco before our mission arrived. These pumps, when all were running, withdrew 24,000 gallons of water per minute from wide, deep holes in the ground called "ains" meaning "eyes" and poured it into a main irrigation canal.

There were a number of these natural cisterns at Al Kharj, each 300 to 400 feet in depth and from 150 to 1,500 feet in diameter. The pits were believed to have been formed first by a slight faulting or torsion in the earth which caused cracks in the sedimentary beds. The cracks were gradually enlarged by the rising waters from below which dissolved the limestone and the gypsum with which many of the sedimentaries are impregnated. Gradually the process formed caverns, the roofs of which finally broke when the span became too great, thus creating open pits. The supply of calciferous water was unlimited and constant pumping never succeeded in seriously lowering the water level.

Our men had built a ladder leading down to the water of the nearest ain, and we all enjoyed a swim that evening and again in the early morning.

The Oasis of Al Kharj

Al Kharj represents the best example of the king's plan to colonize the Bedouin and to make them more self-supporting by the development of agricultural lands. No other reforms are likely to have more far-reaching results.

The king realized, with a vision outstanding in a man who had never been beyond the confines of his own country, that his subjects had to have some central element of stability in their lives if Arabia was to become a united country of good citizens, and that the first step in laying the necessary foundation in the lives of his unsettled nomads, was a home and property of their own. A fixed habitation was unknown to the average Bedouin. Without this tie to bind him he is always on the move and, until recently, lived as much on raids and plunder as by his own herds. Restless and perverse and living by the sword, he was by tradition and custom an enemy of stable government.

Abdul Aziz recognized that the lacking qualities could not be developed in the Bedouin if he led a life governed by his desert code alone. These qualities could only be developed by the order which comes from stable work and from work governed by the order implicit in nature. To him the answer lay in settling the Bedouin on the land. He envisioned permanent settlements as providing not only a means of livelihood but peace and unity by expanding the Bedouin conception of allegiance to their tribe, their community and their state.

The king conceived and organized a special brotherhood which he called the *Ikhwan*. The name means "the brethren united in God." He founded it on the sound principles of allegiance to the purity of the Islamic faith, and the cultivation of the soil. An area of land having wells or springs was assigned in freehold to a group and in time it became their permanent home. The king provided seeds and implements and appointed teachers to train the settlers in animal breeding and agricultural methods. He also appointed religious teachers so as to promote unity of thought and purpose and to spread and strengthen the Wahhabi doctrines. The movement was also intended to provide many thousands of fighting men in time of need.

At first it was difficult to make the Bedouin work systematically or to remain in one place, but they are gradually realizing that in their new existence there is less hunger and more security than in their past order of life. The movement has spread and many colonies have been founded, proving to be a revolutionary measure of the greatest importance.

Formerly the Bedouin knew no worldly ambition beyond the one of the moment to revel for a time in the joys of captured booty. Where formerly each tribe regarded the other with suspicion and envy, constantly engaged in endless blood feuds, and where they depended on robbing the pilgrims to the holy places, they are now brought together in a religious brotherhood of co-operation, social interchange, harvest and economic improvement. Where once they existed on goatmeat and imported rice—undernourished and diseased—they now have begun to thrive on a new diet of fruit, vegetables, meat and grain harvested from their own lands. The *Ikhwan* have proven to be men of uncompromising religious temperament and ruthless fighters. Their one fault is overzealousness when confronted with enemies and infidels.

Al Kharj itself is a model farm, a vivid example of what can be done with soil, water and applied labor while at the same time alleviating the food requirements of the population. Our experts were teaching the Arabs to use modern, scientific farming and irrigation methods. They were raising dates, wheat, barley, alfalfa, various vegetables and an assortment of fruit trees, grapes and nut trees had been imported from America.

The success of the Al Kharj experiment has now inspired the beginning of four additional agricultural demonstration farms in various localities where water is available in sufficient quantity. We have only to consider the similar climate and soil of our own productive western states to realize the unlimited possibilities lying fallow in Arabia; such profound possibilities as will undoubtedly affect to an unknown degree the life and character of that Bedouin nation.

Our men had become lonely and homesick in their strange setting and several declared their intention of returning to a civilized land. With justification they deplored conditions in general and many strange practices and customs in particular. We felt sympathetic to their isolation and deprivations, which were little worse than our own in Jidda; but we could not help being amused at an instance where one of the men was outraged enough to make a report to Washington. He outlined the numerous difficulties but mentioned in particular his aversion to the necessity of associating with a race of people whom he claimed subscribe to barbaric sexual customs. This referred to his discovery that their male cook and another servant were squabbling over the kitchen boy.

This is the only example, in all my experience in Arabia, where such matters came to my attention, although many writers claim that such relationships are common among the Arabs and are frequently the result of friendships which have led to manly affections of depth and force beyond Western comprehension. It is generally believed that these relationships are not uncommon in any of the Middle East countries.

In the Arab world women's influence and accepted purpose in life is limited to the physical world in its most simple form; and this same agreement, by denying equality of sex, makes companionship and love all but impossible between them. It is true that women are regarded as machines for physical pleasure and for the production of heirs and that man's psychic side can be satisfied only amongst his equals. The results are doubtless friendships that attempt to satisfy the human yearning for more than physical contact.

It is sufficient to say that only an overpowering conceit can attempt to explain such manifestations along the lines of abnormal animal instinct. Nor can it be explained by the underlying fault of Moslem philosophy, the notion that women are essentially inferior to men and created to minister to their wants, whims and demands; for unusual sex practices do not seem to be confined nor peculiar to the Arab or Eastern people. More rational causes may be found there but the principal difference seems to be the lack of importance attached to the matter by Eastern races and their uninhibited acceptance of the variety of expressions found to a compelling natural instinct.

CHAPTER FOURTEEN

By Baghdad's Shrines of Fretted Gold

THE next morning one of the men, happy to have our transport, offered to drive us to our rendezvous with the king's plane. We were very glad to bid the truck good-by, but felt sorry to see the last of our companions, even the contrary Ali. We left them with an additional gift, which seemed expected, and in return received their blessings and deep salaams.

The "airport," placed forty miles beyond Riyadh, because no man may look down on that city (as with Mecca and Medina) was a stretch of level desert marked only by a small tent. As we pulled up before it, the silver plane appeared in the eastern sky. After it landed a cavalcade of motor cars began to arrive from the town and at our inquiry the pilot informed us that he was flying the Emir of Dhahran back with us.

The Emir's departure proved a good example of Arab farewells. When an Arab leaves on a trip it seems everyone he can possibly know or be related to appears on the scene. In this case good-by's consumed at least an hour, for every male relative and friend had to kiss and be kissed several times on each cheek and if closely related, a number of times on the lips as well. The crew fussed with the machine and finally started the motors to make them hurry, but nothing succeeded in interfering with the ceremony until completed to everyone's satisfaction.

The pilot, a boy from Nebraska, was called "Little Willie." He had concealed his real age, which was eighteen, and was already a first lieutenant. He was considered one of the best pilots in the Air Force, and doubtless he was, for he had drawn the responsible assignment of flying the king's plane.

The plane, a gift from President Roosevelt, was quite a magnificent affair, deeply carpeted and upholstered in beige and blue. There were plush seats for twenty-one passengers as well as a large built-in double bed and stationary club chair. It was complete with kitchenette and washroom.

The king had not yet flown in it but he had on one occasion sent a number of the women from his harem across country in it. The incident seemed a case of the king's testing such a method of travel before some day attempting it himself. Little Willie said the women had been petrified with fear, but this same fear seemed to extend to others also. Whenever Sheikh Yusuf entered the ship, Little Willie reported that he immediately spread his prayer rug and spent most of the trip in prayerful attitudes, either for public effect or from sheer fright.

The crew delighted in giving him the wrong direction for Mecca, toward which he should have prayed.

The several hundred miles to Dhahran were flown over the continuous red dunes and valleys of the Dahana, its scorching terror seeming but a beautifully tossed sea from the air. We were impressed anew with the wonders of air travel as we considered the days of sweat and labor the crossing would have required by any other means.

Pat and I spent a week in Dhahran, as guests of the American consul and the Arabian American Oil Company; a week which, to us, was sheer luxury.

Dhahran was a new town, built by the oil company on the desolate expanse of the Dammam Dome where oil had first been discovered. It was a completely self-contained community of perhaps one hundred modern cottages and looked like a small California village, transplanted to Arabia. In fact it might be called just that, for every item of lumber, hardware, plumbing and steel needed in its creation had been brought from the United States. The cottages were all air-conditioned, landscaped with flowers, shrubs and green trees. The industrial area contained garages, storehouses, a commissary, a laundry and shops of various kinds as well as the central air-conditioning and power plants. The recreational area consisted of tennis courts, a swimming pool, mess halls, snack-bars, a movie theater and a club house that even boasted a bar. The hospital, company offices and Arab quarters all increased the village to a size where taxis were a necessary means of transport.

The Arabian American Oil Company held concession to an exclusive area of about 440,000 square miles of Arabian territory, an area the size of Texas and California combined. During the early years of the war their geologists had covered 175,000 square miles by preliminary reconnaissance methods and about 50,000 square miles by detailed mapping. Oil had been discovered in quantity in a number of localities but by 1940 only a small, 3,000-barrel refinery was in operation at the nearby site of Ras Tanura. Difficulties created by the war had forced the company to curtail operations, finally closing down this small refinery and, at the time of our visit, they were producing only twelve to fifteen thousand barrels of oil daily. This was transported to Bahrein Island which lay just off the coast and perhaps twenty-five miles from Dhahran. It was refined there by the Bahrein Petroleum Company Limited, a company owned by Standard Oil of California.

Despite the war problems of material shortages, personnel and shipping, it had become evident in Washington that foreign sources of oil must be made quickly available. The tremendous drain upon the dwindling American oil reserves, caused by the war, was of such serious concern to our government that a foreign oil-expansion program had been formulated by the Petroleum Administration for War. This agency was organizing and directing the prodigious efforts of the oil industry to meet the vast demands of the Allied military forces and of our own industrial production.

Aramco had just received approval for the construction of a 50,000-barrel per day refinery at Ras Tanura and the area was in the usual pandemonium of activity that accompanies any such major construction project. A submarine pipe line was being laid to the Bahrein refinery, which was also in the process of expansion. Construction camps with all their supporting facilities were springing up here and there and thousands of Arabs were being trained in the various jobs connected with construction work and oil production. The new refinery involved new storage tanks, loading lines and a long pier and wharf. High military priorities were being assigned to the many critical materials required and the military authorities were co-operating in the movement of men and materials, all of which were under their control and allocation.

It was extremely difficult for Pat and me to realize we were still in Arabia. In one short day we had been transported from the feudal court of the Lord of Arabia, across two thousand years of time, to a modern industrial world. It was incredible. We gorged ourselves on wholesome American food, watched American movies and lounged about the Hollywood swimming pool, trying to comprehend it all.

The face of this eastern part of Saudi Arabia was being changed just as fast as men and machines could operate, but the matter went far beyond that. Thousands of Arab youths and adults were attending company schools where they were learning to read and write and acquire various skills. After a life of idleness they were now working eight hours a day, earning money, eating regularly, wearing better clothes and living more comfortably. Their health as well as their living standard was being improved. All these benefits extended to their families and on to the merchants, craftsmen and builders who served them and supplied their wants. It was a movement that would in time affect the entire nation, but what impressed us more than looking into the future was the fact that given the opportunity, the training and incentive, the Saudi Arab was not too proud nor lazy to work. He was proving himself to be an apt pupil and as capable of accomplishment as any other race. It was apparent that Arabia was moving rapidly into a new era, an era which might match, if not excel, the accomplishments of its long and glorious past.

After a week at Dhahran, and when plane seats were obtained, a launch took Pat and me to the island of Bahrein where we boarded a huge British flying boat. As night fell we settled on the waters of the Tigris at Basra where we intended to spend the night. We walked into the rambling Shatt-al-Arab Hotel to find the lobby crowded with

British soldiers listening to the stirring V-E Day address of Winston Churchill.

Making for our rooms we bumped into Dickie, one of our British members whom we had left in Jidda. Dickie was responsible for the British side of our transport program and was as completely British as the equipment he managed. His short figure was dressed in regulation khaki shorts and shirt and he had added an Arab beard to match his blond English mustache. He was a very silent person with the disconcerting habit of listening but rarely offering a reply. He inspired one's sympathy, for he never laughed and seldom smiled, yet seemed less unhappy than lost in introspective thought. One might be inspired with friendliness toward Dickie but he seemed lacking in any similar response, which may have been only his natural British reticence.

Recovering from our mutual surprise in seeing each other, Dickie informed us that he had flown over to bring back a convoy of 250 trucks turned over to the Saudi government by our United States Army Persian Gulf Command. He surprised us further by insisting that we celebrate V-E Day.

That evening we dressed in Arab robes and began our celebration of the inspiring news with a bottle of the best champagne the hotel had to offer. It proved to be Russian, vile in taste and even worse in aftereffect. We then visited several native "night clubs," conspicuous in our robes and headdress which everyone recognized to be that of the royal Wahhabi family. It did guarantee respect and service as well as padded bills.

Next morning Pat and I took our horrible hangovers along with us to Baghdad. Taxying along the palm-fringed Tigris reminded me of Tennyson's poem:

> "When the breeze of a joyful dawn blew free
> In the silken sail of infancy,

By Baghdad's Shrines of Fretted Gold

The tide of time flow'd back with me,
The forward-flowing tide of time;
And many a sheeny summer-morn,
Adown the Tigris I was borne,
By Baghdad's shrines of fretted gold,
High-walled gardens green and old; . . . ."

The next stop was upon the salty waters of the Dead Sea where we tarried long enough for a plunge in the hard brine. The celebrated columnist, Dorothy Thompson, boarded the flying-boat here and shared our cabin to Cairo; while we discussed with enthusiasm the war, the question of Palestine and the Middle East in general.

With the dusk we settled, like a homing duck, upon the Nile and proceeded at once to Mena House Hotel at the foot of the Giza Pyramids. The servants salaamed and greeted us with broad, welcoming smiles, making us feel as though we had returned home, for it was indeed home to me. Here I had lived, preceding the assignment to Arabia.

The tiring trip was a compelling reason for a good drink and cleansing bath, so we went immediately to our room. It was my own old room, spacious and cool. Its latticed, Swiss balcony overlooked the tea gardens and framed the towering Cheops close by.

During the week at Mena we tried to be very sporting and carefree. After once making lengthy reports at the office we assiduously avoided it and spent the time dashing about town to clubs, parties, the races at Gizera, dances, dinners at the Auberge des Pyramides; seeing old friends and trying to forget during it all, the war and Arabia in particular. With Eleanor there it was wonderful for Pat, but for me the return to Egypt's luxuries somehow seemed dull and senseless. The fun seemed forced and Cairo's gaiety as foolish as the antics of an ostrich, for the decisive struggles of the war had not ended.

The scene had shifted since my Cairo days. The masses of troops —American, British, Indian—had swept on to attack the very heart of the trouble, leaving even Cairo a backwater. Yet the tempo of social life had increased, as if determined to ignore the European havoc wrought by the war. I felt a strange longing for the contentment and way of the desert, where one's life and destiny somehow seemed more ordered and controlled.

One moonlight evening I climbed alone up the hill from Mena to the base of Cheops, the great pyramid, around it and down to the feet of the Sphinx on the other side. The long hill rose behind to the towering Chephren, weirdly illumined in pale yellow light. Here I had last said good-by, so long ago. I rested on the sand, to gaze again in silent awe upon the immutable stone face; upon a serenity past understanding.

The Sphinx should only be seen in soft, golden moonlight when his ancient domain is mysteriously still and deserted. Then the inscrutable face becomes alive. The facial highspots gleam palely, the eyes and throat remaining in shadow and the battle scars of centuries healed from view. Only then might be glimpsed his patient, faint smile of esoteric wisdom carried from some forgotten age—more provocative than that of the Mona Lisa. It is a superior, impersonal expression of tolerance and understanding beyond the grasp of mortal mankind.

If one is sensitive to the desert whispers that softly move about the great expanse of sleeping tombs, and quietly studies the moonlit brow, he might discern something of his elusive secret. One thinks he has guessed it, but then it is gone, for it is intangible, incomprehensible. The intent gaze of the Sphinx remains fixed upon the eastern horizon, waiting for the reappearance of his supreme deity, Ra-Harakhti. Expectancy and confidence are chiseled there too, for only the Sphinx remembers how many days, how many thousands of years he has unfailingly greeted the rising sun while the fortunes and follies of men rose and fell, and how many more will inevitably follow. His secrets are guarded, as are those his spell falsely inspires, whispered in the enchantment of his recumbent shadow.

Pat and I boarded an RAF plane one morning just as dawn crept over the Nile Valley. The take-off was quick and in a few moments we climbed into the sky over Giza, above the ground mist that hid the ribbon of lush green valley below. The mist clung to the valley, bordered by the golden desert, and only the peaks of the three great pyramids pierced the veil and towered above it.

The experiences of the past month were to me like the pyramids of Giza. They pierced the ground mist of every-day living. They were as towers among my days.

CHAPTER FIFTEEN

Where'er I Roam

THE servants crowded the doorway to watch my unpacking. Ibrahim's expectant grin reminded me of an Egyptian *dragoman*'s when he sees the Alexandria train disgorging crowds of defenseless tourists for his plucking. Even Hamid broke into a covetous smile when I opened a bag revealing my Cairo purchases. As I unpacked I mimicked in a crying falsetto voice directed toward Ibrahim,

"*Gib baksheesh, gib baksheesh, ana meskeen!* No mamma, no pappa, no brother, no sister, *ana meskeen!* (The cry of beggars in Egypt: "Give alms, give alms. I am poor!") The servants howled with laughter, appreciating the butt of the joke.

It was wonderful to be home, to have been missed and welcomed back again. Even blasé Donald was happy enough to frisk about, wagging his silly-looking tail and kicking up his heels. I grabbed him by all four legs and swung him over my head and around my neck like a fur piece. He enjoyed it and the grinning dark faces marveled how I could do anything with him when no one else would be permitted to even lift him without a fierce struggle. He did not thresh or resist but hung about my neck as supple as a well-fed kitten. Putting him down it occurred to me that I had thought of Jidda as home. This would never have been possible a few months before but now I felt held in a glow of peace and contentment unknown before. I was at last approaching the heart of Arabia, the heart of a simple and sincere people.

The luggage contained some little thing for each of my watching audience and, though it may have been only an inexpensive article, being new and shiny and American was enough for it to be preciously received with loud thanks and eloquent *"al hamdu l'illah's."* Each was made happy and content with his simple treasure. Each, except Ibrahim, who tarried hopefully for more until being forcibly ejected from the room.

Donald was no less curious than the servants. In fact he far exceeded them in enthusiasm. I could not unpack fast enough to please him, so he took the matter into his own hands and carefully inspected each article as it lay in the open bag. First one fine-smelling thing after another captured his interest. He picked up a package of cigarettes but before making off with it, the bright wrappers of candy bars attracted his eye. The cigarettes were abandoned for a candy bar and this in turn was quickly rejected in favor of something else. He became frantic with delight and indecision until obliged to settle down in the open bag, atop his treasures and toys and with them scattered distractingly about him.

"Ah *maleesh!*" I cried, giving him a rough hug. "I know who lost my watch, you little rascal, but I don't care! What's a watch? The king has plenty more. Do whatever you like, any mischief you can think of, and I'll not spank you. At least for a week," I provided, rumpling his head. To this he merely flicked his tail and tossed his head in a winsome gesture of independence.

When I started for the office below, Donald scampered along behind me. Before leaping to the *roshan* he pranced about, arching his neck and enjoying the feel and jingle of a new collar. The substitute friends of my absence were ignored in the pleasure of my return.

The *roshan* was a built-in settee that extended along the wall and used for Arab comfort in discussing business. The gazelle liked to pose or recline upon it while I worked at my desk since it gave him an elevated view of all activities both in and out of the office.

Before settling down to consider the eccentricities of mankind and the speculative chewing of cud, Donald first pawed the selected spot very thoroughly. When it was suitably worked up and then stomped down again, he bent first one front leg under then the other as he descended head first to his knees. In this half-way position, with tail in the air, it occurred to him that everything was not quite perfect. While striving at a decision, he maintained his ludicrous pose, lolling a wad of cud from one side to another in bovine reflection. A decision was finally reached. He arose to make several indolent circles and to face another direction, then progressed to the stage where he again rested on his chin. It still was not right. Disgusted with the fuss entailed in comfort, he jumped up to stalk stolidly to the other end where he flopped without even a preliminary inspection, folded his legs beneath him, sighed contentedly and started the machinery working for the job of transferring breakfast from one stomach to another.

I smiled at his evident pleasure in the return to our old routine, and for some reason Goldsmith's words came back to me:

"Where'er I roam, whatever realms to see,
My heart untravell'd fondly turns to thee;"

PART III

CHAPTER SIXTEEN

King John and His Slave Hamid

OUR organization was also our household. We worked together, lived, ate, played and drank together. Everything was done as a family but, thank Allah, we at least slept alone; each man by himself, except for his dreams, his memories, his hopes—cherished in secret like hoarded gold sovereigns.

Millions of assorted, diversified personalities were placed on the wheel of chance and the hand of fate pointed each of us out; calling us from here and there, away from our work, families and friends, to perform a particular function in the disaster of war. It placed us, complete with our virtues and vices, together on the desolate sands of

Arabia. Some before us had failed in spirit or health or by some good fortune were suddenly remembered by headquarters and transferred elsewhere.

Fred and I, civilians, found our lots thrown in with three young British majors—Pat, Frank and Dickie—thus setting the stage for the daily trial of the four cardinal virtues so well distinguished by Plato as prudence, fortitude, temperance and justice. This trick of fate was a full deal but she overdealt the cards when she threw John in also.

John rivaled Ibrahim in many respects. His skin was very thin, in one sense only, and very white since he disliked going out in the sun. He referred at every opportunity to his illustrious sire, a judge in Edinburgh. He may have been only a small-town constable, for nothing else, unless it were John's abnormal size, could explain his innate inferiority complex.

This complex was carefully secreted beneath an irritating exterior of overbearing pompousness and verbosity, aided and abetted by a resounding, sonorous voice, purposely pitched in a key designed to vibrate one's nervous system like a tuning-fork and to crack glasses in the next room with its penetrating resonance. He had diligently practiced and developed the art of his voice, probably not to be deliberately annoying, but to save himself steps and to insure an abundance of prompt service, for no matter where the servants might have been, they could not avoid hearing him—nor could we. They responded with alacrity and, although John liked to believe it was because he impressed them, they actually had little respect for him and small regard for his orders. The sole exception was old Hamid, for he made the original mistake of being awed by John who then maintained a stranglehold on the poor man's primitive senses. In slave-Hamid, King John found his abject subject and the scenes which occurred between them were like something from Gilbert and Sullivan.

John liked to hold court in his office immediately after satisfying his cultivated but unrefined appetite at a large and extended breakfast. He bellowed for Ahmed and for Hamid, as well as any other servants he might wish to grant audience. They appeared from wherever they might be to find John seated in ease and importance behind his desk, blowing smoke from a large cigar and enjoying his tenth cup of coffee.

John denied them even a glance, but as Hamid crept in, without a sound in his straw slippers, and stood meek and trembling with hands clasped behind him as though waiting for the fall of the headsman's axe, John spoke to Ahmed, while indicating Hamid with a grandilo- quent sweep of his cigar, "Inform this *man, . . .*" he began in a pompous voice.

Rising from his desk, he took a grand turn around the room and started over, gesture and all, "Inform this *fellow* . . . that in fu- ture . . . , etc. etc. . . . or he shall be dismissed forth*with!*"— BANG! on the desk for emphasis, causing both Hamid and the coffee cup to jump, one from his old slippers and the other from its saucer.

From the adjoining office I could see Hamid quaking and looking as if he might burst into tears. We, overhearing, would not have been surprised to hear John pronounce an *Alice-in-Wonderland* verdict of, "*Off* with their heads—every one of them!"

John was referred to by all who knew him as "dear" John. But he was not without virtue. He possessed a good mind, which was his own undoing, for although he had a smattering knowledge of a great many things, it caused him to venture garrulously upon any given subject whatsoever and in presumptuous style to orate and expound outrageous facts, theories and figures as if picturing himself a Winston Churchill addressing the House of Commons.

One learned, knowing John, not to be so impressed as to accept without question these innumerable dissertations, which were intended for psychological effect only. In time one perceived that many of John's astounding quotations were lacking in authenticity and that where he was so often unqualified or uninformed, he was not beyond manufacturing, with brazen facility, facts and figures from thin air as required to fit the circumstances.

John did, however, possess an extensive knowledge of Egyptology, his best subject. But even here he was mighty careless about throwing dates around, thinking nothing of being a thousand years off one way or another but stoutly maintaining his position until a Baedeker should be produced to prove him wrong. One was compelled to prove him in error occasionally, but when pointed out in black and white, John was capable of dismissing the matter as "doubtless a mistake on the part of Baedeker or the *World Almanac!*" But I did enjoy discussing ancient Egyptian history with John, providing I disregarded his authoritative statements where I knew him to be wrong.

As John loathed all forms of exercise not involving a knife and fork, he was forced to invent substituting interests. Fortified by a fertile imagination this necessity presented no undue problem and he succeeded in formulating a variety of stimulating diversions—usually involving the fluctuations of the local exchange. He performed no work whatever beyond ordering unappetising meals of lamb curry, his responsibilities seeming to handle themselves in due course.

One was often prepared to murder John, but he was invariably saved by the armor of his facile tongue and impressive self-possession. Neither he nor Ibrahim would ever venture out fishing with me and I often wondered if they actually disliked the sport or if they mistrusted me.

My tolerance can be questioned, however, without recording the fact that I was the only one, beside Fred, who was civil to John. I sometimes took him for a ride when the sun moved toward evening; the time for Donald's daily run on the desert, although he was nervous about straying far from the beaten tracks.

One afternoon, when we were both feeling unusually depressed and morbid, I prevailed upon John to break his record and go for a walk. We decided to explore south of the town where no one ever ventured since it led through the obnoxious city dump, past the putrifying odor of the local abattoir and bands of ferocious *pariah* dogs gone wild.

We were armed with staves so none approached in the daylight to attack us but followed at a discreet distance like hungry wolves. They were filthy, emaciated, horrifying creatures and in the chaotic locality seemed heinous spirits of hell.

In this unlovely setting we came upon a walled enclosure and entering through an iron gate found it to be the Christian cemetery. It was more desolate and neglected than the tombs of Upper Egypt and only intensified our depression so that we could have sat down and wept.

There were perhaps fifty graves in all, many of them so old and crumbling as to be undiscernible except for the remains of a headstone fast returning to the surrounding dust. We found one lonely stone cross on which could be deciphered:

"James. . . . . . . .42–1762. . . . .at sea. . . . . . .age 18. . plague. . . . .H.M.S. . . . . .peace."

The vision of the crew coming ashore to bury their young comrade in the burning waste so far from his loved ones almost overwhelmed us. To change the scene John suggested in his booming voice, "Well, Bob. Better pick out your little plot of sand!"

But I vowed I'd never lie in that distant God-forsaken place.

On another occasion John accompanied Donald and me to the so-called Tomb of Eve which lies beyond the Mecca Gate. The name Jidda (Jeddah) means grandmother, and the town was so named no doubt in honor of the mother of the human race who is supposed to be interred there. She must have presented a very peculiar appearance when alive, however, for two low parallel walls eighteen feet apart and two hundred paces long define the depression where the mortal remains of our giant mother is supposed to rest. There too is seen a tremendous stone slab, and it is interesting to note that the archaeologists record that the great idol of Jidda in the age of Arab litholatry was a "long stone."

CHAPTER SEVENTEEN

Encounters with the Outside World

OUR principal contact with the outside world was represented by the ATC plane that hesitated at Jidda on its occasional flight to Asmara in Eritrea. It brought our mail sacks and sometimes a visitor and was not only a visible proof of a world beyond those burnt shores, but a reassuring promise of eventual escape.

Its arrival constituted the one small weekly or bi-monthly excitement. When the droning motors were heard overhead everyone with transport rushed out to the smoothed area beyond town where it landed; some to receive diplomatic mail but others with only the hope of seeing a new or familiar face. It was a keen disappointment to find the plane empty or carrying no mail. However, it usually carried at least some strangers headed for ports across the sea. They were welcomed, accepted as friends and plied with questions. When one of us departed in the plane, even for only a short leave, the incident was often an emotional experience and we became as bad as the Arabs in the length of our farewells.

The other contact, but a less exciting one, consisted of two small ships which handled the Red Sea trade for the Isthmian Steamship Line. They operated between Jidda and Egypt and their bi-monthly visit was only less exciting because they did not actually arrive in Jidda but anchored far out to sea. They brought all the supplies and equipment, trans-shipped from America, for which we were responsible. This battered cargo was moved from the ship to the quay in crude Arab dhows which often lost some of it overboard on the perilous trip through the reefs. It was incredible what loads they could carry and what colossal crates they sometimes brought in, all moved by hand after once being swung from the ship's derricks. Often two dhows were tied together to accommodate oversized crates or trucks. These were often placed so precariously—perhaps hanging over into the water or only a few inches above it—that I could hardly bear watching their uneasy progress shoreward.

The dhows tied up to the low stone quay built parallel to the shore-line. Shabby but cavernous storage sheds and a rambling customshouse fenced in the wide quayside. The cargo was offloaded by half-naked, chanting crews of black skeletons of men. They were Takrunis and Somalis, bossed by Arab crewmasters. Many of them were bonded slaves. No mechanical device was available to help in the unloading, so even the crates containing trucks, automobiles and heavy equipment were all handled somehow by the cheaper human labor.

It required two men to swing a large box or bale from the dhow to the turbaned black head of a waiting slave. When properly balanced he trotted off, and I watched, expecting his spindly legs to buckle and snap from the unbelievable load under which he staggered. One might wonder how such wrecks of oppressed humanity could sing, but their chanting helped them. It gave them courage and created a smoothness of unified effort. Without it they would have been powerless.

The noise and confusion on the quay was as saturately complete as the desolation of the desert was absolute. Gangs of dockworkers were crowded to the water's edge by the tangle of wagons and carts pulled by teams of small donkeys. Camels snarled protestingly while kneeling to be loaded with sacks of spilling grain or torn bales of textiles. The commotion created heavy clouds of dust that appeared as localized *simooms*. Their billowing density was increased by the ever-present swarms of persistent black flies which caused seeing to be as difficult as breathing. A veiling *qhotra* was never more necessary than in that stifling pest hole, that suffocating hell of hot bodies and angry animals.

The Isthmian ships also brought our food supplies, ordered from the United States or England. The perishables were flown down from Egypt, which tripled their cost. However, we were mostly dependent on British Army (NAAFI) supplies. They were of poor quality to begin with and the months in transit did not improve them. The flour was thickly inhabited by weevils when it reached Jidda and the brown sugar might contain anything.

Though expensive and of damaged quality, we were nevertheless grateful for the privilege of receiving these supplies. We felt that the British at least knew and cared that we were on the job, and that could not be said for the United States Army Chief of Staff for the Middle East Command. For many months that pompous gentleman denied us even a meager PX privilege in Cairo. This meant that we did without all the small things that make life bearable at such posts. If possible he would have denied the diplomatic personnel in Cairo the same privilege, but he did succeed in making them enter through the rear door on one specific day only.

But these things were only typical of my entire war experience. The British never failed in an emergency and always extended a gallant hand whenever the aid of our own people was refused. This was no reflection on our own army personnel but strictly the result of un-American, discriminatory top policy in Cairo, as everyone realized. The social whirl of Cairo and life among the palatial villas along the Nile permitted them little vision beyond the frail ambitions of their own brief moment.

Nearly all food for Arabia must still be imported, with the exception of meat. Goat meat is the steady diet but camel and beef are sometimes available also. One learned not to inquire as to what he was eating but rather to eat it with gratitude and hope for the best.

A few green vegetables and tomatoes occasionally found their way to the *suq* and were either grown in local wadis or imported from Eritrea. During certain seasons figs, pomegranates, prickly pears and grapes were brought down from the Taif district in the mountainous interior. Displayed in the market, however, their covering of flies rendered them hardly attractive enough for eating. Otherwise, unless subscribing to the Arab diet of meat and rice, we were dependent on canned supplies.

All these small things brought a gradual awareness of Arab philosophy, from which we perforce borrowed rather generously, and *maleesh* assumed a practical meaning.

CHAPTER EIGHTEEN

If God Wills

WE AWAKENED one morning to the rare sight of an American freighter anchored in the outer harbor. It brought a great shipment of materials for the Saudi government, all of which came under our aid program, and kept me happily busy for nearly a week. The captain was a fishing enthusiast, so when the unloading approached completion I offered to take him out in the Red Sea for an afternoon's sport.

After the necessary arrangements were made Sayed placed my boxes of food and tackle aboard the weathered crate engaged as a motor launch. I boarded the craft from the low stone quay, polished to a slippery smoothness by the bare feet of millions of landing pilgrims, and, to a chorus of Arab good-wishes, shoved her toward the open channel.

One of the two Arab boatmen crouched amidship encouraging the uncertain motor, while the other stood forward carefully steering through the shallow channel that ran first one way and then another, avoiding the coral ridges submerged just below the blue surface. They were cheerful brown fellows with curly dark hair, flashing black eyes and strong white teeth—pleasant of feature and disposition. As soon as we cleared the inner lagoon they stripped off their sarongs, converting them into turbans as protection from the piercing sun, and in only cotton shorts exposed their lean muscular brown bodies to the hot sea breeze.

The freighter lay deep in the water several miles offshore. Arab dhows were lined at her side waiting for the remaining grain, looking like young ducks huddled about their mother for protection.

An Arab foreman superintended the busy unloading by streams of lusty orders to his chanting Takruni crew. To the loud clatter of ship booms the cargo was swung overside to the waiting dhows below. When the battered dhows were loaded to the point where one more sack of grain would swamp them, they shoved off to wallow heavily until a favorable breeze billowed out their high patched sails. When able to move, they rushed in at a dangerous keel, through the treacherous shoals which every dhow master knew with his eyes closed. If the wind suddenly died, animation deserted them and their drooping, fluttering sails had to be quickly furled or changed in tack before leading them aground on the sharp coral banks.

We approached the freighter's side and as a long swell lifted the launch high, I jumped for the ladder and climbed to the deck above, where Captain Henry awaited me. From this elevation we obtained a good view of Jidda, deceivingly large and impressive looking. It was a dazzling white beneath the blazing sky and was sinuously reflected in the broad lagoon.

Captain Henry descended the swaying ladder with me to the bobbing launch below. We cast off and headed seaward for the breach in the barrier reef.

The tackle, of my own devising, amused the captain, but I had found through experience that it was impractical to use anything in the Red Sea in the way of standard equipment. It was not possible to buy rods and reels locally, nor anything else sufficiently heavy for the game which inhabited the deep waters beyond the reef. One might troll for smaller fish but even a light feather lure would be struck by the larger fish, always resulting in the loss of tackle. It is said that more sharks live in the Red Sea than any other waters on the globe. Immediately on hooking a fish of manageable size, it is always seized by one of these mammoth brutes. Consequently, one is fortunate to retrieve his tackle or at best to haul in only the head of his strike.

My solution to the problem was to be prepared for the sharks with the very heaviest hand tackle. I had welded two large hooks together, braced by a steel bracket and set in a steel shaft sheathed in white feathers. The heavy steel wire leader was attached to a strong linen handline. It seemed capable of holding a whale or at least of pulling me overboard before breaking. It was awkward, however, to play a catch without rod and reel, and my burns and cuts testified to the difficulty as well.

As soon as we passed through the narrow channel into the deeper, dark water, we cast our lines astern and began to troll slowly, perhaps fifty yards beyond the reef. The great swells rolled our craft gently then swept on to crash like muffled thunder upon the submerged barrier.

Captain Henry at once had a strike and I realized it to be a barracuda. The specie in the Red Sea strike hard but lose fight when hooked. As the boatman idled the motor Captain Henry drew it in close enough to gaff. Severe clubbing finally stilled the snapping jaws which were lined with double rows of sharp teeth, and we judged it to be about four feet long.

Unfortunately the next strike was mine. Although it burned my gloved hand, I succeeded in checking its run while yelling, *"Stana Shawa! Stana Shawa!"* to the boys. ("Stop," or "Wait awhile.") I had played it but a few moments when it surfaced near enough for me to see that it was a huge "tunny" of perhaps one hundred pounds. At that moment several large dorsal fins suddenly cut the water in close pursuit. In great excitement I hauled fast on the heavy line, not permitting the tunny chance for a run. Our first catch had attracted the sharks and I knew they would follow from then on.

I managed to bring the tunny close to the boat when a large gray shape appeared beneath him. I called for the gaff and almost fell overboard in excitement, terrified that the shark might get him. The shark shot in suddenly then almost lazily rolled over on its side. Its great toothed white jaw closed in a voracious snap on my luckless fish. They almost took me over the side before their combined weight snapped the line, letting me fall backward into the launch.

Much provoked, I ordered the boys to proceed and only then noticed that the motor had stalled. The action with the tunny had consumed only a few moments but already the ocean swells had carried our craft much nearer the reef. The boys, easily excited, worked furiously at the unwilling motor with only a sputtering response. Captain Henry ran forward and cast the anchor overboard to check our drift. It dragged alarmingly before catching, then its rope snapped like a string.

The boys were now too frightened to be of much service and, losing their heads completely, kept changing places with each other, between the wheel and the motor. Their panic only increased our peril.

Each wash lifted us yards nearer the reef as we stared helplessly. Even the boatmen ceased their efforts and stood spellbound, staring toward the sea-covered coral. My heart leaped to pound in my throat as several high black fins, attached to mammoth dark shapes, lanced the water close by. One reared from the deep to yawn in our faces, exposing its wide pink throat and saberlike teeth. One of the boys recoiled, covered his face and moaned in terror. We tensed ourselves, holding to the ridge pole. We intended to jump if the boat capsized and make for the high point of the reef where the water might be too shallow for the sharks.

The next breaker lifted the boat high, held it for a moment then flung it with a crash against the reef. It rolled on its broken side and quickly filled with water, but we clung to the high gunwale for our lives as the boat seemed to cling to the coral for its own.

I was no longer conscious of any personal fear. I understood only a terrified determination that nothing should go to the savage beasts loitering about us. The barracuda began to float over the submerged gunwale and my senses seized upon it. *"Ana samek!"* I yelled, and to the nearest boy I gave a command in tones he dared not disobey.

He broke from his terrified muteness. *"Allah! Allah! Shufti—kebir samek!"* he screamed in defense. I looked where he pointed to see a dark head rise above the water. With an ugly crunch it closed on the barracuda to disappear in the swirling darkness.

Each succeeding breaker battered our craft further upon the grating coral, threatening each time to shatter it to pieces. The sharks slid through each wave without effort, remaining close as if waiting to be fed. We searched the sea for another boat or some unnamed miracle to save us, but it remained void of all except ourselves. Nothing rewarded our hopeful gaze but an angry expanse of dark water, faintly outlined by a low brown ridge on the so distant horizon.

After several hours the pounding surf succeeded in lifting our battered launch by slow stages almost across the reef and presented the added danger of pushing it off into deep water on the other side. In such an event the smashed hull would sink like a rock and the tenacious sharks receive their reward. The frightened boys moaned and sobbed to Allah for deliverance. To reassure them, as well as ourselves, I borrowed from their own philosophy and promised we would be saved —God willing!

If Captain Henry learned any Arabic it must have been *"insha' Allah,"* for our every thought and utterance was tempered with this overworked phrase which we learned to employ as frequently as did the Arabs.

The fiery sun began to sink toward the western edge of sea, casting a burnished red glow upon the water. With a shock I saw our chances diminish as each moment the space of blue between sun and sea became smaller and smaller. My mind raced here and there seeking some bit of hope to fasten on, refusing to accept the fact that only an hour remained and that no one could ever find us in the great waste of darkness soon to descend. Luckily much time was consumed in an attempt to remain with the lashing wreckage, but during lulls our inaudible prayers were added to the blatant ones of our despairing boys.

A sudden excited cry from one of them roused me. I thought his cry of *"sambook! sambook!"* merely a crazed utterance, for we could see nothing. He pointed toward a small island, barely visible in the dim distance. The island was used by the Saudi government as a quarantine station during the periods of pilgrimage and was inhabited by one lone Arab and his dog. It would have been wildest wishing to hope that he might see our wreck and attempt a rescue.

Refusing any false hope, we peered ahead, withholding our judgment until a small white sail did actually emerge through the haze. Then with beating hearts we watched as if our gaze might draw it to us.

The small sail glided forward with enraging slowness, promising little hope of rescue before the darkness blotted us out. The sun hung ready for its final plunge into the molten sea when it became possible to see that the craft was a native *hoorie* with rigged sail. We gripped the gunwale, watching. Silently it glided near just as darkness fell with the abrupt suddenness of an extinguished light. Its boatman called a greeting and I at once experienced a flood of fondness for him. The boys could not suppress their joy and relief and to their repeated *"al hamdu l'illah's"* I added my own.

The boatman was the keeper of the quarantine isle and he explained that only by the grace of Allah had he chanced to sweep the sea with his glass and spotted our wreckage clinging to the reef.

We thankfully abandoned our broken and sinking launch as it clung to its last grasp of coral, reluctant to sink to a final resting place. Carefully we laid our tired bodies close together on the slimy wet bottom of the overloaded *hoorie*. The hazardous craft held us all but our danger was far from past. After removing the sail to prevent swamping, the keeper carefully paddled for the more placid lagoons. The smallest wave or slightest movement might have turned us over, so we lay still, scarcely breathing as the penetrating cold and dampness settled like a death shroud upon us.

Late in the night we reached the Jidda quay and helpful Arabs lifted us, stiff and cold from the confining *hoorie*. Through chattering teeth I joined in another weak but grateful *"al hamdu l'illah!"* Captain Henry promised the boys they should have enough lumber from his ship to build several launches. He had been a good sport but as I bade him good-night it seemed evident his enthusiasm for fishing had been somewhat dampened.

Ibrahim was waiting at the door when I reached home. When he saw me empty-handed, he shook his head, turbaned for once in a clean white *qhotra*.

"What, no *samek?*" he asked as I stumbled in.

Sensing his understanding of a familiar situation, I wearily replied, *"La, Ibrahim, mafeesh samek."* Then in self-defense I added, "I did hook a great big one—but he got away!"

CHAPTER NINETEEN

Powers of Suggestion

IN VARIOUS Oriental cities the bazaars or market places bear different names. In Algiers there is the Kasbah, in Cairo the Mousky, in Damascus The Street Called Straight, but in Jidda no such romantic or mysterious name applies. Only the short *"suq"* that perhaps is suitable enough.

There I bought rugs as some women buy hats; purely for reasons of morale and furthermore because there was little else worth buying. One missed in some ways the convenience of stores but it was an entertaining pastime to wander through the *suq*, visiting stalls here and there and inspecting any new rugs that appeared from time to time. The bargaining for and final acquisition of a rug afforded an uplift in morale as well as an esthetic pleasure in obtaining something new and

· *167*

beautiful to add to one's quarters and feast his eyes upon.

Rugs reached the market by devious means, sometimes being offered for sale by Jiddawis who had held them as an investment, or else brought into the country by arriving pilgrims from the far eastern corners of the Moslem world. Not only did they serve their useful purpose on the pilgrimage, but they were always a tangible asset easily disposed of when money ran short, or at the completion of the *Hajj* when the pilgrim was ready to depart. He rarely left with anything of value but was plucked clean by the Jiddawis and Meccans who thrive on the pilgrim traffic like heartless parasites.

The *suq* was entered through a nearby gate, its high frame erected of coral rag cemented together and covered with white plaster. The huge double doors were of thick, heavy teakwood, grayed with age and sagging on their rusty antique hinges. The *suq* began as a wide open market place, but within a short distance narrowed to no more than a covered alley. This, and a similar passage that intersected it, was shaded by sackcloth awnings and matting, patched here and there like a Bedou tent. Through its gaps and tears shafts of sunlight pierced the fetid gloom, appearing like solid columns of dancing dust and swarms of flies. The motionless hot air seemed a physical thing through which one pushed his way. It was necessary to keep fanning with a flybrush or handkerchief to prevent the flies from settling in a sticky, persistent layer. They crawled in such deep numbers over the few pitiful displays of fruit and vegetables that it was difficult to determine the produce beneath.

In all of Jidda, only in the *suq* was there activity and masses of people. Only there was heard the babble of many voices and the sounds of animals. Growling, complaining camels and patient, docile donkeys followed their masters stolidly through the motley lot. The effect was exciting as I threaded my way through the dense crowd of Bedouin

Sudanis, Somalis, Indians and Javanese, in their diversified and colorful costumes. Many were ragged and dirty, some dressed in simple smocks with scarves tied about their middles or turbaned about their heads. Yet many were dressed as prosperous merchants in gowns of white silk, and others as desert princes in fine camelwool *mishlahs* and cashmere headcloths. Most of the shopkeepers wore white broadcloth *thobs* that reached the ground but gave a glimpse of embroidered ankle-length drawers beneath. On their heads were either small round *kufis,* exquisitely stitched in designs of gold and silver thread, or starched, white linen caps. The scene was completely masculine, for women do not appear in public in Arabia. The occasional female figure encased in black might be a beggar of low caste, perhaps blind and led by a small black child.

The stalls and small shops on either side were like miniature stages, raised a foot or two above the damp ground. Seated Arab fashion upon the rug-covered floor, the shopkeeper sipped Turkish coffee or sweet mint tea, entertaining friends or customers and enjoying the custom which we called *fadling,*—the endless exchange of courtesies. His goods hung in chaos on the surrounding walls or was piled in corners, and toward the front might be several small showcases of odds and ends, knick-knacks and religious souvenirs.

The small shops catered to every variety of Eastern requirement and my progress was accompanied by a passion of smells, drifting from acrid sweat and urine to roasting coffee and baking bread—the smell of the East that cannot be analyzed. It is animal and earthy, full of spice touched with musk and wholly intoxicating.

Money-changers occupied corner stalls, seated among their chests of assorted monies, constantly clicking stacks of silver riyals from one hand to the other while calling forth the day's quotations on gold sovereigns and Egyptian pounds.

Only once did I stroll as far as the meat stalls with their nauseous smells and unappetizing displays of fly-blackened goat or camel meat. My one ambition was to release a DDT bomb in the place but Fred always dissuaded me.

It was more interesting to visit the crafts section where some weaving was done, and to watch the dexterity of the silversmiths and metal workers with their crude and primitive equipment of the type used since the beginning of time in that ancient land.

I paused one day at the shop of Mahmood, the rug dealer, for his quick eye had caught me some distance away and, knowing my weakness, he was already holding out an ochre and blue Bokhara to arrest my interest. At his suave invitation I sat down and accepted a small coffee from his servant. Mahmood was jovial and as fat as only a successful town dweller could be. A thin white cotton *ihran* rested on his black oily hair and hung down either side his cunning face. Minus the *agal* (headropes) and following the practice of touching up the eyes with black *kohl,* he seemed a ludicrous actor, enjoying to the full his particular lazy role in our human comedy.

After enough discussion to appear civilized, I finally consented to the rug being sent home on trial. I would live with it, hoping Donald might not eat the fringe as we carried the bargaining into weeks of negotiation. It would probably be sent back and forth a number of times before we reached a satisfactory figure, although even then Mahmood would have the final advantage.

As I proceeded each acquaintance called forth a greeting and an invitation to fadl, but it was necessary to pretend an urgent engagement. Otherwise the day would be wasted in idle tea drinking and the nights made sleepless in an unbearable agony of physical longing, for their cardamom tea is an aphrodisiac, perhaps a necessary part of an Arab's diet who has the peace and contentment of his harem to consider.

Beside his religion, which is so much a natural part of his life as to be unconscious habit, the Arab has room in his head but for three things. His major interests are in food, the acquisition of money and that quaint pastime that is regulated by the size of his harem and his physical condition. These interests do not necessarily fall in the order named, but his devotion to the latter assumes the proportions of fanatic zeal. His appetite is keenly whetted by the interesting promises of the Koran, and he is ever alert to possibilities for increasing his natural ability.

In Arab countries doctors are besieged by men seeking some medicine that will increase and intensify their sexual capacity. The aging and ailing want a tonic that will restore them to youthful virility and those still in their prime want a medicine that will preserve and increase their desires and stamina. They do not fear death as they do a diminution of their reproductive endurance, and it becomes a serious matter of pride with them as well.

Whenever I met Aziz, who happened to be a wealthy and educated merchant, he never failed to broach the subject of the marvelous medical discoveries recently made as related to glands, agents of rejuvenation and increased virility. He felt certain that in America I could obtain for him some of the new hormone serums or something even more potent, which he apparently expected to multiply his prowess to that of the Bull of Bashan. He was a huge, healthy specimen, simply radiating lust, and had no need, I felt sure, for such artificial aids. I asked him why he wanted such obviously needless and powerful stimulants.

"Oh," he cried, "I visit my harem every day, but why should I not have such pleasure more often, or perhaps take another wife, to the glory of Allah and the propagation of our race?!"

"Yes, why not?" I said.

He urged me to think of some modern American miracle capsule, so I asked if he had ever tried vitamin E, this being the first thing to enter my mind.

"No, but is it any good?"

"Aziz, it is the most wonderful thing in modern times," I invented, "and guaranteed to produce the most desirable results!"

Since Aziz seemed enchanted with the news, I foolishly enlarged upon the virtues of vitamin E and suggested, to please him, that he send for a sample. He at once dictated a cable to his *effendi* (clerk) ordering ten thousand capsules, to be shipped air express by his New York connection.

Feeling as if I had inadvertently started a flood of vitamins sweeping the desert of Arabia, with results perhaps too horrible to imagine, I attempted to escape, but Aziz held me, asking if I had a few on hand which could be spared until his order arrived. One foolish mistake led to another. I hesitantly said that I had, fearful of any results, good or poor which might or might not follow. However, Zaid carried a small supply over to him later, as I had promised.

We chanced to meet again on this particular day and on seeing me, Aziz swept me off my feet. As the crowd looked on he clutched me in his massive arms and, while crushing a few ribs, planted a hearty kiss on either cheek.

"Bob, you are my friend!" he exclaimed, putting me down. "*Al hamdu l'illah!* Only an American product could be so marvelous!"

Shaken and disheveled I looked at him in some astonishment, but he went on to elucidate, "You know, Bob, the first day I took four vitamins, and I assure you, they are positively wonderful! Now I shall take another wife."

It required a full mustering of self-control to refrain from the disillusioning comment that vitamin X or a capsule of bicarb might have achieved the very same result.

CHAPTER TWENTY

The Fast of Ramadan

ALTHOUGH the year was 1945 elsewhere, in Arabia it was 1364 by the Moslem lunar calendar and the month was *Ramadan*.

Ramadan is second in importance only to *Dhul-Hijja,* the month of pilgrimage. All Moslems the world over must observe the thirty days of Ramadan by severe fasting. Unless deathly ill, they have no choice in the matter. Otherwise, strict observance is unconditionally compulsory. As prescribed by the Prophet, they may not take food or liquid after the hour of dawn when a white thread and a dark thread held before one at arm's length become distinguishable. All through the hot and thirsty day they may not take one drop of water nor a morsel of food until the light fails and a white thread and a dark one cannot be distinguished one from the other. When this happens they may then quench their thirst and take food to relieve the pangs of hunger.

In Jidda these hours were officially announced by the firing of the old cannon out at the barracks. When its blast trembled the buildings the town suddenly became alive, as if shaken from its stupor.

The purpose of the fast is discipline. It is intended to teach the Faithful lessons of privation and discomfort and to reduce all, rich and poor alike, to the same level through common suffering. And they do seem to suffer a great deal. It must be a severe test of faith, especially to those who must work, to endure the burning desire for water all through the torrid day. Many of the more fanatical will not even swallow their own spittle. To the great masses the nights of Ramadan have become times for feasting. It seems a human failing to be more conscious of the need for food when strictly denied it. As a result more food and liquids are consumed during the hours of darkness than would ordinarily be taken during daylight.

In all Moslem countries the working classes play up their misery during Ramadan to obtain the fullest possible measure of sympathy and leniency in their work. Servants drag themselves through the day, threatening to expire at any moment right before one's unpitying eyes. It is actually a great farce on their part, for if they would only eat at night and retire like normal beings they might at least be as fit as they ever are. But instead, they dramatize the matter and spend most of the night in feasting and celebration, getting little or no rest.

As they must also abstain from sexual indulgence, the nights, when not spent in eating and drinking, are conscientiously devoted to this pleasure as if it were about to be permanently removed from them. My understanding operated quite normally I thought, but my tolerance became strained under the circumstances, especially when the servants moped about, neglecting their work and protesting their disability under the guise of religious devotion. If I asked Ibrahim to run a short errand, he assumed a posture and expression that indicated his serious doubt as to whether or not his strength would permit it. I always made him go, however, recalling the fact that the servants' quarters resounded with hilarity until three each morning.

The Moslem creed in its simplicity and as established by the Prophet, is composed of the following precepts:

1. Belief in God. There is no God but Allah and Mohammed is His Prophet.

2. Belief in God's angels. There are four principal angels: Gabriel, who is the medium of revelation; Azrael, who receives the souls of the dead; Azrafel, the trumpeter; and Michael, in whose care is entrusted all created human beings.

3. Belief in His Books. Allah is believed to have revealed many sacred books to the prophets from Adam down. All are believed lost except Mohammed's Koran, the Gospel of Jesus, the Pentateuch of Moses and the Psalms of David.

4. Belief in His Prophets. Moslems are taught that God has sent many thousands of prophets since the time of creation. The greatest of them all were Adam, Noah, Abraham, Moses, Jesus and Mohammed. (It should be noted that Jesus is considered a prophet.) Prophets are believed free of sin and Jesus was the purest of them all. Mohammed refers to Jesus as the Spirit of God and the Word of God, but never as the Son of God.

5. Belief in the resurrection and the last day of judgment. The approaching day of judgment will be preceded by the return of Jesus. He will die again, and it is said that a place is reserved for his burial beside Mohammed in Medina.

6. Belief in the predestination of good and evil. Allah's will explains everything that has happened or will happen, all that has been and all

that ever will be. (This is the origin of Moslem fatalism.)

Under this creed Mohammed outlined five specific duties:

1. The most important duty is the pilgrimage to Mecca. The only followers exempt from this are those for whom it is a physical impossibility because of ill health or lack of funds.

2. Strict observance of the major fast of Ramadan. (There are other fasts as well.)

3. Recital of the creed. In simplicity this amounts to, "I believe there is no God but Allah and that Mohammed is His Prophet."

4. Prayer five times each day—before dawn, at noon, midafternoon, sunset and again two hours later.

5. The giving of alms. One fortieth of all gains should be given to the poor and needy. One day in the year is specified for this occasion although alms should also be given throughout the year. Devout Moslems are exceptionally conscientious in their observance of this rule.

It is a very simple religion but not an easy one. The obligations of Islam are extremely demanding. There are the prayers to be observed, the fasts, the pilgrimage and the almsgiving. It does not appeal to the spiritually lazy nor to the selfish and it furnishes no outward show or worldly reward. But it is a practical religion and perfectly adapted for the people and conditions of Mohammed's time—conditions which are only now beginning to change.

The Allah of Islam is not someone to whom one turns in times of distress but an always present, benevolent spirit. He is not beseeched for favors but constantly praised for His daily blessings and the help which will always be extended as He sees best. The spirit of Islam is a spirit of brotherhood, of liberty, equality and fraternity as authored by Christ. The Arab is an individualist in the highest sense of the word, and under Islam he continues to worship these virtues more fervently than is done in any other land. Islam agrees best with the Arab's nature, for whom it was conceived. His relation to God is a personal one, for there are no priests or intermediaries, only instructors. It contains the active quality of making God the very real and actual being of whom the Arab is always conscious.

The occasions in the Moslem calendar that would be equivalent to our holidays have by custom become days for gift-giving. The poorer classes who benefit have grown so accustomed to the practice that they not only expect presents or money, but the more degenerate in large cities demand it as their right. It has been carried by many among the servant class to the extreme where they also expect *baksheesh* on our own Christian holidays as well. It has become such a common practice as to cause them to lose sight of the fact that gifts are made by one's own free will, out of the kindness or generosity of one's heart, regardless of the exhortations of the Prophet. Instead, many servants in Moslem countries demand these gifts as their inalienable right.

Ibrahim never failed to demand his *baksheesh* on every holiday with which he had acquainted himself, including my own birthday. I often reminded him that it was *my* birthday or *our* Christmas; not his, and that I expected a present on such occasions. This always amused him. He grinned inanely and gaily muttered, *"La! la!"* as if he detected in me a case of arrested development, or at best found me possessing only a childish sense of humor.

On leaving one's employ all servants expect a generous parting gift as well as a glowing written testimonial praising their virtues to near sainthood. It was often difficult to oblige in regard to the latter, but fortunately none of them read. I felt certain Ibrahim for one, labored under no illusions, however, for I promised that any recommendation from me would contain the truth and at least insure his incarceration.

In the Prophet's homeland nine children out of ten are named after him. Many are named after the calendar month in which they are born, that particular month becoming their own, like a name-day. At one time we had a driver named Rabi, after the month of February. At another time, when living in a houseboat on the Nile, the young cook, as impossible as old Hamid, was named Ramadan.

I shall never forget Ramadan. He was unbalanced enough to rival some of the exploits of many of my American friends. We were very happy eventually to release him to work for some of these friends, where his entertainment value was ranked above his ability to cook. These friends were assigned to the Naval Attaché's office and I learned, with complete understanding, that life after acquiring Ramadan, never suffered a single dull moment.

They once gave a large stag party and arranged through Ramadan for a group of Egyptian entertainers to amuse the guests after dinner. The entertainers arrived in due course and put on as boring a show as the guests could endure. One dull vocal number followed another until one of the fellows named Sam anxiously inquired of Ramadan when the real show would ever begin. The surprised Ramadan replied that Sam was watching the show—what did he mean? Sam impatiently elucidated his first question with, "When the hell do they start to undress?"

It developed that they were not going to undress, for Ramadan had not engaged that sort of talent. I was well acquainted with his devilish sense of humor. However, he maintained that he had understood Sam to say the guests would be very respectable married ladies and gentlemen and that the entertainment must be fittingly restrained. Of course Sam had tried to say exactly the opposite; but as he was just learning Arabic, it is possible Ramadan did misunderstand him.

Some time after this an American friend of mine arrived in Cairo. Marj was the lovliest girl the city of beautiful women had seen in a long while, so quite naturally these same fellows lost no time in their clamor to arrange a suitable welcoming party. Sam again ordered the perverse Ramadan to secure the services of some entertainers—and not to make a second mistake this time. Their guest of honor was a most proper and respectable young lady and the entertainment must be such as not to offend her.

Our amusement (or chagrin) can well be imagined when later in the evening the first of the troupe slunk into the spotlight to perform her dance. To the wail of a single flute she enthusiastically launched into a sensuous undulation that was locally known as a "belly-dance" —in nothing whatever except a very fragile wisp of tulle!

PART IV

CHAPTER TWENTY-ONE

Vice Is a Monster

V-J Day was cause for rejoicing and celebration in Jidda, as it was in all parts of the world. We decided it was our particular day to go the limit and give the largest party we could possibly arrange. Every Christian in Jidda, as well as a number of westernized Moslems were invited. Our food stocks were in good shape and we had recently received a substantial liquor shipment, so were well prepared to give everyone all they could eat and drink.

Servants were never a problem on these occasions. They simply came of their own volition from every other establishment in town, to participate in the work and spoils. The kitchen looked like the hold of a pilgrim ship, with servants either preparing dishes or gathered in solid masses of black and white along the walls to watch the others.

After the last guest should depart they would form circles on the floor, around communal bowls containing all the left-overs which they might eat by Moslem law.

Fadl was by this time our chief cook and very excellent too, being especially accomplished in preparing fish dishes as delicious as they were elaborate. Fortunately Hamid, like Ana meskeen, considerately disappeared, so we were spared the pain of sacking him. He did not mysteriously disappear, but asked for leave to visit Mecca, and nothing was ever heard of him again. Perhaps the emotional experience was too much for the old man, but we were never able to find out.

The food was served buffet style from a long table as abundantly filled as any in Egypt. Fadl turned out masterpieces of roast beef (probably *gamoose* or water buffalo) roast turkey from Eritrea, *bayad* in aspic, fish mayonnaise, mountains of *pilau* (rice with fish, fowl or mutton) hot breads, *sambusa,* Arab cheeses and various other delicacies the ingredients for which could be found in the *suq*. The king could not have set a finer table, a fact which made Fadl beam in modest self-satisfaction.

Good servants like Fadl took a personal interest in all phases of one's social life, considering it of the utmost importance that proper impressions were made and that all entertaining be above criticism. Otherwise it proved a reflection upon themselves and an embarrassment before their friends.

We improvised a bar by placing several desks together and had the servants beg, borrow or steal ice cubes from every house that boasted a refrigerator and a plant to run it. Fred decided to concoct a V-J cocktail for the more hearty few who never seemed able to slack their thirst. He emptied into a large jug the remains of every opened bottle in our collection. Proportions were unimportant; everything was simply dumped in and stirred up with ice added. The many bottles represented a surprising variety of alcoholic beverages which in combination were a startling experience for our guests. A bottle of ketchup was added to lend color and to act as a cutting agent. To me it tasted like battery acid or something the Russians might serve, and we hardly thought that anyone, except possibly John, would suffer more than a taste and that even he would accuse us of trying to poison him.

The cocktail proved so popular however, that everyone demanded more, being unaware of the ingredients, and we were able to dispose gracefully of several unpalatable bottles of liqueurs some enterprising Palestinians had foisted on us. At least they had the good effect of breaking everyone down to a very sociable state without undue delay.

John ate the entire supply of pear-halves stuffed with cheese, which he had ridiculed as "preposterously American," when in the preparation stage, and was, I am happy to record, constipated for an entire week. Conventions and inhibitions became so relaxed that several guests went completely native, whatever that may mean; and Harry Mayhorn from Aramco, unaware of his latent talent, put on a brilliant sword dance with a young Arab sheikh!

Since Donald was as sociably-minded as any of us, it was not possible to keep him locked up; an act neither he nor the guests would have permitted. As usual he was friendly and entertaining. He met everyone at the door, inspected them until recognized, then relieved them at the first opportunity of any cigarettes within reach. He helped himself to a drink as soon as a glass was found unattended and drained it dry. It led me to suspect that he had been drawing a ration from Dickie or John all along. The drink produced such frolicsome gaiety as to make him the life of the party. He performed capers unmatched before.

Donald first experimented with his favorite game of matching strength against someone's foot. Meeting a little resistance pleased him so well that he leaped into the air, tossed his head and executed the gymnastic feats of a circus clown. His footing gradually became less sure as he tired or became dizzy until, when dropping his head to a butting position, his front feet slid slowly apart until he rested in a comical pose on his chin. In this ridiculous posture he thoughtfully considered the matter, then, rising slowly to his feet, stood blinking in supercilious dignity as if some unfathomable trick had been played upon him. I stopped the performance at this point with a rewarding plate of food hoping it would have a sobering effect.

Should anyone suspect that foreign service in such spots as Jidda might constitute a "lost week-end," they may be assured that such is not the case. With the help of Melottis gin from Eritrea, service there usually amounted to one perpetual lost week-end. More than one claimed this was the only positive method of combating the numerous germs encountered each day and the only insurance for keeping well. The proponents of this theory proceeded to prove it, and the theory possessed some virtue. It seemed best confirmed by those who drank the least for they were actually ill the most.

The party was such a complete success I am certain there could not have been an ache-free head the next morning. I took several aspirin for my own relief, and on being accusingly observed by Donald gave him one as well. He chewed it thoughtfully, waiting to be brushed and reflecting upon his social accomplishments while I considered his particular ways.

Donald was as fastidious about his person as he was about food. While it is true he liked a diversified diet, from carbon paper, book covers and cigarettes to everything I ate myself, he nevertheless would not touch anything that was soiled or had been near one's mouth. He could not be tricked, and he refused with a snort the most tempting morsel if it had once been bitten into. His tendencies toward vice were all human-inspired.

V-J Day was over and I forbade anyone to ever slip Donald a drink. For the doubtful edification of John and Dickie, as well as Donald, I recited for them from Pope, to the effect,

> Vice is a monster of so frightful mien
> As to be hated, needs but to be seen;
> But seen too oft, familiar with her face,
> We first endure, then pity, then embrace.

CHAPTER TWENTY-TWO

Beginning of the Pilgrimage

EACH night the gangs of wild pariah dogs descended on the city from their camping grounds outside the wall. They took over the territory which they would not invade during daylight, and raced through the streets in such howling gangs as to prevent sleep, had the heat permitted any. After they had slaughtered a few of themselves and moved on to other parts, sleep of a kind became possible. But it was of short duration. Suddenly the compelling boom of a baritone voice sounded below my window. It often caused me to almost jump through the mosquito netting.

The Jidda mullah paused below the house of unbelievers to utter in an impassioned roar, *"La ilaha illa Al-lah 'Mohammedun Rasulu Allah!"*—"There is no God but Allah, Mohammed is His Messenger."

It was a great temptation to drop something on his holy head, for many times, after tossing all night in the wet, enveloping heat, sleep was just arriving when he ardently commanded, *"Allahu Akbar!"*—"God is omnipotent." *"Heiya 'ala-ssalah!"*—"Come to prayer."

Nevertheless, the call was so inspiring I half consciously awaited it. Although sufficient to wake the dead, its appealing beauty, heralding a new day, shall never be forgotten.

They said the old *mullah* was insane, a rumor which seemed true, but he might only have been possessed of an uncontrollable religious fervor expressed in the self-appointed task of waking all Jidda each morning for the betterment of their souls. We were not the only ones he startled with his sudden vociferation that rivaled John's best, and at least one other sufferer put my own threats into effect. He always bellowed beneath the window of Amrullah Bey, of the Turkish Legation, until Amrullah threatened to correct such misdirected zeal in one way or another. Of course he could take some action without consequence, being a Moslem, but I never could since I was an infidel.

When Amrullah could endure the disturbance no longer he waited one morning for the *mullah,* and as the old man paused below, filling his lungs for the long aria, a bucket of cold water suddenly descended upon him. He ran screaming in drenched surprise and ever after avoided at least one sinful soul in Jidda.

Another distraction about this time were the pilgrims camped around our house. They began to arrive for the *Hajj,* which is performed during the twelfth month, *Dhul-Hijja,* of the Moslem lunar year, as all true believers have done for more than thirteen centuries. The poorer *Hajjis* could not afford to live in hostels but camped in the streets; cooking, eating and sleeping there in the dust until transportation could be secured to Mecca. Some had made the journey slowly from the far places of Africa and from the many countries of the Middle East. All faithful, able-bodied Moslems who can possibly afford it must make the journey to the holy city of Mecca at least once in their lifetime. They work, live and save with that one consuming hope in mind and when at last foot is actually set on holy soil they are overwhelmed in the realization of their dreams.

The *Hajj* is intended primarily as a memorable historical pageant, staged annually to keep alive in the minds of all Moslems the memories of past events. Its importance can hardly be overestimated. It unites Islam as no other thing could, for at Mecca the Javanese meets the Negro from Senegal and the mountaineer from Spain, all brought together by the same holy purpose, in a remarkable community of religious dedication.

The *Hajj* is one of the oldest ceremonies in the world and has a ritual of organization dating from centuries back. Endless complicated requirements and prohibitions are prescribed. Women may cover their heads but men may not. It is the only time women may go unveiled. If they do, however, unbelievers may not look upon them without offense and possible injury to themselves. To cover the instep is forbidden and certain sects, which seems a contradiction, require that the men's beards be hennaed to an unnatural carrot-red.

As many as 280,000 *Hajjis* are said to have arrived in one year, but the average number is between eighty and one hundred twenty thousand. Because of the war and difficulties of travel only forty to sixty thousand were expected this year; but even such a number represented a tremendous passage of people through a little town of normally twenty-five thousand.

The greater number arrived in Jidda by steamers chartered for the pilgrim traffic. These ships brought men, women and children from the East Indies, India and in times of peace even from Japan, Russia and the most inaccessible provinces of China. Ships of many countries, British, Dutch and French, waited to take them back to Algiers, Capetown, Singapore, Zanzibar and Alexandria. They arrived packed like sheep, most of them spending the long voyage living on deck, performing all functions there as they did in our yards. Many others traveled thousands of miles across Africa or down from Iraq, Iran, Afghanistan and more remote places; by foot or by camel, stopping enroute when necessary to earn a little money to carry them further. To perish on the way meant merit in heaven, but to succumb in the holy land itself was like getting a through ticket straight into paradise.

Agents in the Moslem countries book the pilgrims' passage to Jidda and if desired, consign them to representatives or licensed guides who call themselves *mutawwifs*. The pilgrim enters the sacred zone when the city is sighted, and must then begin the complex rituals of ceremonial initiation, first removing all ordinary clothes and donning *"el Ihram"* which means "mortification," the prescribed dress for the *Hajj*. It consists of two lengths of toweling, one wound about the waist and the other over the back, gathered at the right side and leaving the right arm exposed. It is purposely seamless to avoid the suggestion of pretense.

For the pilgrim the Koran prescribes, "Let him have neither commerce with women, nor fornication, nor a quarrel on the pilgrimage." Religious instructors advise him to avoid quarrels, abusive language, light conversation and all immorality and to religiously repect the sanctuary of Mecca by avoiding to destroy plant or animal life; excepting, however, the five nuisances—a crow, a kite, a rat, a scorpion and a biting dog. He is advised to abstain from all washes, perfumes, oils, dyes and cosmetics, the paring of nails, the cutting or plucking of hair and the tieing of knots in his garments. Each infraction of these ordinances require the sacrificing of a sheep or goat.

The pilgrim prostrates himself in ritual prayers, facing Mecca, until the ship drops anchor. *Sambuk* and dhow skippers crowd round to bargain transport to the quay and the *mutawwifs* scream up to the lined railing to identify their customers or secure additional ones. From this moment until he leaves the holy shores, the pilgrim is at the mercy of the Jiddawis and Meccans, for their principal industry is still that of fleecing him. Up until the recent discovery of oil the only state revenue was derived from heavy pilgrim fees.

When the ship's ladder is lowered everyone rushes pell-mell for disembarkation, shouting and yelling in such pandemonium it seems families and baggage would never become united again. Men, women and children go over the side, clutching water jugs, pots and pans, squawking fowls, boxes and bundles, while the heavier baggage is swung over their heads to the dhows below. As the overloaded craft rush in through the coral reefs each pilgrim is posed on his prayer rug in a state of religious fervor, suddenly absorbed in his beads and prayers.

He is landed on the quay and proceeds through customs, followed by a perfunctory quarantine inspection and accompanied through it all by the same wild confusion and disorder, flies and filth. His papers must be found in order, he must be free of any noticeable communicable disease, he must pay the head tax of four gold sovereigns and he must satisfy the authorities beyond doubt that he is indeed one of the Faithful. If not detained or deported he might eventually find himself out in the dusty, noisy street, surrounded by a bedlam of animals, people and piles of goods and chattels.

When guides, families and luggage are eventually united they trudge through the crowds to one of the many hostels waiting as traps set for their victims. The hostels are only bare, empty rooms. Otherwise they set up housekeeping in the confusion and dust as if on a deserted prairie, until moving on toward Mecca. Every drop of water must be purchased, at a now regulated but still high price. The pilgrim will find no facilities of even the simplest kind provided for his comfort or convenience but he will find the avaricious Jiddawis determined he shall not escape with one remaining *girsh!*

Many pilgrims are crowded into ancient dilapidated busses for transport inland, with baggage piled so heavily on top one catches his breath on seeing them sway round a curve. The fare is high, forcing many to travel by camel or cheaper still, by foot. The amusing part of the bus arrangement is that the passenger is charged for either a first-class or second-class accommodation. Nevertheless, all are packed so tightly together without distinction, that they hang precariously from windows. Busses often break down on the desert. If Mecca bound, passengers are forced to complete the trip by foot, but if Medina bound, many in years past have been known to perish on the hot sands.

Camel caravans were loaded in our back yard day and night during the *Hajj.* To the soprano chatter of women and the guttural tones of men were added the rough snarls and gurgling growls of ill-tempered camels. After abiding the sounds of these beasts for so long, I reached the conclusion that the original Arabs must have learned to talk through constant association with their camels, which probably came first. During the night when their complaining became subdued through fatigue, it was difficult to determine whether the throaty sounds rising to my room were produced by men or animals. Many of the strange Arabic sounds, which cannot be reproduced in English, were no doubt borrowed from these monstrous creatures.

When ready to load, the cameleers beat their charges over the head with camel-sticks, yelling, *"Ikh! Ikh!"* to make them kneel. Wide, flimsy bamboo frames, canopied with matting or sacking, were placed upon the protesting animals' backs, and a kick in the ribs accompanied by, *"Yahh! Yahh!"* brought them quickly to their feet for fastening of the girth straps. Several men and women then crawled into each of the rickety, swaying perches, along with their baggage, by means of a flimsy ladder placed against the animal's withers. The cameleer, meanwhile, firmly held the beast's indignant head to prevent his reaching around to bite the frightened, screaming passenger. This seemed the most common of the camel's many vicious tricks against anyone he dislikes, which appeared to include everyone within reach and even Donald and me as we secretly watched at our window.

The loading was accomplished by raucous, contradictory orders shouted above the tumult of hysterical women and snarling beasts. When completed, the desert pullmans were roped together in lines of six each and with the cautioning, *"Hai! Hai!"* were led away, more to our relief than that of the courageous pilgrims. To their annoyance the caravans dawdled outside the Mecca Gate until at last formed into long cavalcades for the weary forty-hour trip to the holy city.

I was always impressed with the fact that it must be a very passionate religious devotion that would compel these poor souls to attempt such a perilous journey under such rigorous conditions. Yet it goes on year after year. If they survive the torture of heat and the rough ride, a gale is liable to end them by blowing the *howdah* off and casting them head-on to the rocks and sand below.

I was interested to learn the truth about conditions in that microcosmic capital of Islam. It is the religion that brings together and amalgamates all the heterogeneous constituents of Meccan life, and this society welds into a chaotic whole the prejudices and superstitions of all countries. It is natural that the mixture of religious fanatics from many races and over the centuries would not be conducive to good morals, and beyond question it is true that up until the reign of Abdul Aziz, the immoral reputation of Mecca was fully deserved. During the rule of the Turks all travelers and writers testified to "the flagrant immorality that pervaded the streets and even the mosque of the sacred city; the prevalence of the slave trade, the fleecing of pilgrims and corruption of the government."

Before the advent of Abdul Aziz, Arabia was torn by tribal feuds; banditry and pillaging by the nomadic people were recognized vocations, and no roads, herds or travelers were safe. When tribes were not warring with one another they were raiding and slaughtering the pilgrims. In their guardianship of the holy places the *Hijazis* had distorted the Prophet's teachings, making corruption and immorality the order of the day.

Before the king could apply religious reform he first had to establish obedience to law and order. By ruthless enforcement of Sharia Law and exemplary administration of justice, he gradually reduced banditry to a scale smaller than that in perhaps any other civilized country. Every subject realizes that a loving but stern monarch watches all corners of his empire and that nothing escapes his notice. He knows the penalty for theft is the quick loss of his right hand and that men are beheaded for worse crimes.

When law and order became established the king assembled a Moslem congress for the purpose of giving to all the opportunity to suggest appropriate measures for cleansing religious observances and the restoration of Islam to its original purity. Although he has asked for and accepted the co-operation of the religious leaders in this respect, he has always retained the political administration of the country under his exclusive control.

The pilgrimage can now be made in safety and the stranger is secure providing he is not an unbeliever and wanders into forbidden areas. Slavery has been reduced, the price of a slave alone being prohibitive now. Enforcement of Koranic laws regarding crime and adultery is so severe that offenders are rare. They know that the penalty may be quick death. The king's stern rule has reduced the traditional practices of favoritism and corruption in the government as well as improving the lot of the pilgrim. Guides, cameleers and hostel-keepers are supposed to work on scheduled prices and today the pilgrim may secure redress in the courts in cases of extortion or neglect.

Although Mecca itself may have been named the sink-hole of Islam in the past, it is now no more wicked or corrupt than any other Eastern city; and as for the country as a whole, the new Arabia enjoys more security and a lower crime rate than any other country in the world. This is due alone to the strength of Abdul Aziz and the wisdom of his reforms.

CHAPTER TWENTY-THREE

The Navel of the World

THE subject of Mecca, the *Kaaba* and its sacred Black Stone, the pilgrimage and its complicated rituals, has for so many centuries held the interest of the world that a number of writers have attempted to broaden the limited knowledge available. Since 1853 Sir Richard Burton's account has been considered the most authentic and accurate one. However, although his account, like that of others, speaks with most emphatic exactness, it too contains elements of error. When writing about the most sacred emblem in Islam, the Black Stone, Burton claimed that it was encased in a block of solid gold. This is as untrue as are the sequence of rituals that he is believed to have observed in person.

Although we lived within an hour's drive of Mecca and often

ventured to within sight of the city, I shall not make the claim of having been there. The situation did afford me opportunities for gathering enough first-hand information, however, as to make its recording a necessary part of these notes.

Mecca nestles so secluded among the arid, rocky hills that the pilgrim does not realize his approach to it. From out of the infinite expanse of burning sand and blackened rocks, he suddenly comes upon the high, crenelated wall and, as if in a dream, approaches the guarded, fortress-like gate with its triple arches and rounded tower abutments. He is caught up in the flow of humanity and carried through the portal, adding his own shouts of joy to the chorus, "Here am I, O God, at Thy command!"

The city in which he finds himself is the home of 100,000 people. It lies in a sandy wadi, enclosed by hills that are void of any verdure whatever. The wadi is long but very narrow, so that houses have gradually crept up the surrounding slopes until it appears like a stadium. Destructive floods often tear down the narrow valley, inundating the city, destroying or damaging everything in their path. The great mosque, *Mesjid el Haram,* lies in the bed of the wadi, in the center of the city, and all the unpaved streets slope toward it so that it stands as it were, in the pit of a Greek theater.

Mecca exists today just as it did before Mohammed's time. Its narrow, winding streets are the same, and, where time and heat have crumbled buildings into dust, similar houses have been built on the ruins of the old. Instead of dying like other ancient cities, it continues to live, rising higher and higher through the centuries upon the recrement of its own decay. The people are just the same, as are their dress and customs. Meccans still consider themselves the most cultured, and their spoken Arabic is still the closest approach to the classical.

The city was a sacred place of pilgrimage and a busy caravan center for hundreds of years, even before the days of Mohammed. Because of this it always has been wealthy, the pilgrims alone bringing in great sums of money each year. It is a city of large durable houses and hostels built of brick mixed with granite and sandstone and of the same interesting architecture as Jidda. Surprisingly, it boasts of one hotel reputedly as palatial as Shepheards in Cairo, where the Eastern potentates and extremely rich of the Far East, along with their retinues, are quartered in accustomed luxury. The most notable visitors, however, are usually quartered by the king's invitation at his Meccan palace.

If an unbeliever should ever succeed in reaching this forbidden area, especially during the *Hajj*, he would be torn apart by the infuriated mobs. Scarcely a pilgrimage took place in the past without some persons being killed by the *Hajjis* or put to death as intruding Christians.

A pilgrim from Iran lost his life during my first year in Arabia. He became sick in the holy *Kaaba* and but for the intervention of the police would have been torn to pieces on the spot. Feeling ran so high against the man, who was thought to have intentionally defiled the shrine, that the pilgrims could be placated only by his official execution. Iran severed diplomatic relations over the incident and they have not yet been renewed. Because of this Iranians have not been allowed by the government to make the *Hajj* since.

The black-draped *Kaaba—Beit Allah* or House of God—stands in the vast central square of the Mesjid el Haram mosque. The four sides of the mosque that form the square consist of an uncountable number of columns, nineteen gates and six stately minarets. All unoccupied ground is covered by pavements and graveled spaces where prayers are said, each sect having its own allotted space. At no time, day or night, is this place ever wholly deserted. Beside the *Kaaba,* a number of minor structures dot the courtyard. A high pulpit stands nearby and from it thousands of Moslems are led in noonday prayers on Friday, the Moslem Sabbath, and opposite it is the Zemzem well. Tradition says that Hagar, cast into the desert with her son Ishmael, thrust him under a bush to die where she could not see him. As she wandered in the burning desert, a voice directed her to the Zemzem well ("the murmuring") and she and her child were saved.

When the Zemzem water is dashed over the pilgrim it causes sins to fall from his soul like dust. If there is any merit in this belief, then we should have been quite thoroughly purified for often we had nothing better to drink. However, this most sacred and historic of all earth's waters has been quite unjustly maligned. It is only slightly saline and if cold is much better tasting than the condenser water of Jidda which is only wet and nothing more.

The *Kaaba* square is the center of the universe to all Moslems. They believe it stands directly beneath the throne of God and they refer to it as "the navel of the world." It is said that the most careless never contemplates it for the first time without fear and awe.

"*Kaaba*" signifies a cube and although the temple's measurements do not quite justify it, the best description is to say that it is a square structure, very large and exceedingly plain. Each of its four sides are of varying dimensions, but it is approximately thirty-five feet in height, width and length and is built flat-topped of massive basalt blocks of unequal size. There is only one high narrow entrance door, made of aloe wood. It is opened ten or twelve times each year under the guardianship of the Bani Shaiba family—the hereditary holders of the key by divine decree. The Faithful who can afford the price of admission enter the building in suffocating masses by means of a ramp that is moved up to the door. It is said that scrupulous Moslems do not willingly enter as they may never afterwards walk about barefooted, take up fire with their fingers nor tell lies. Few of even my Meccan friends had ever ventured into the House itself; if for these reasons, I do not know.

An annual present of gold and rich tapestries is sent by various Moslem countries to the Grand Sherif of Mecca. It is carried as a covered litter and called the *Mahmal*. The one from Egypt always included a beautiful new silk and cotton covering for the *Kaaba* called the *Kiswa*. In 1926, however, an incident happened on the plains of Arafat that interrupted this practice. The fanatical Ikhwan resented the presence of the Egyptian *Mahmal* and the sounding of their bugles on this holiest of soils. They began to stone the *Mahmal* and this led to the exchange of shots. Fifty camels and twenty-four men were slain in the fracas that followed. It would have resulted in even a worse slaughter but for the intervention of the king, Abdul Aziz. This was during his first visit to Mecca.

Although the Ikhwan had started the trouble, the Egyptians were guests in Arabia and the place was sacred. The Egyptians were, therefore, as much at fault as the Wahhabis. The king in the highest wrath of which he is capable chastised them without mercy and the result was the discontinuance of the Egyptian *Mahmal*. It was sent only once since that time until very recently when Egypt finally forgot the matter sufficiently to resume sending the *Kiswa* regularly each year. It is carried in a great procession all the way from Cairo, leaving there with much ceremony on one of the great feast days and arriving in Mecca in time for the *Hajj*. It is made in sections to fit the building like a shroud and is inscribed in deep bands of gold thread bearing the words, "Verily, the first house founded for mankind to worship in is surely that at Mecca, a blessing and a guidance to the world," and seven other short *suras* from the Koran.

The section of the *Kiswa* which covers the side of the *Kaaba* pierced by the door is called the *Burqa*. It is a rich veil of silk like the other three sides but has a slit for the door and is heavily embroidered in gold arabesque. The faded *Kiswa* from the preceding year is cut into small pieces and eagerly bought as religious souvenirs.

The *Kaaba* was a sacred temple even before Mohammed and its retention in Islam is an obvious anachronism. According to Moslem teaching, Abraham was the father of the Faithful and it was he who originally built the structure as a house of worship in the spot designated by Gabriel when the angel handed him the sacred Black Stone. Still other legends state that it was the original home of Adam and Eve and that Abraham merely rebuilt it.

The building was cleansed of pagan idols by Mohammed in the sixth century and although it was once the repository of priceless treasure, nothing could be more simple than its interior today. The walls are hung with handsome red damask, flowered over with gold and tucked up beyond the pilgrim's reach; and many lamps, said to be gold, suspend from the high ceiling.

Near one corner of the *Kaaba* is inserted the Yamani Stone which perhaps is often confused with the Black Stone. This relic is a broken but mended block of gray granite whose history is lost in antiquity. Nothing seems to be known about it except that it figures in the ritual. When possible for the pilgrim to approach close enough, he must touch the stone in a downward gesture each time in passing on his course of the circuits. As the crowds are always too dense for any but a few to touch it, this rite may be accomplished simply by a salutation from the distance.

The most venerated Moslem object is the *Hajar el Aswad*, or Black Stone. This is one of several controversial subjects so definitely yet so erroneously described by even those who claimed in the past to have seen it.

This antiquity is fixed in the southeastern corner of the *Kaaba* about chest-high from the ground. From the surface it appears as if fifteen fragments had been bound closely together, although this may only be the peculiar formation of the material of which it is composed—a variety of quartz. The diameter of its surface is about seven inches. It is black, glossy and pitchlike, and polished by myriads of osculations through the centuries. It is encased in an oval frame of solid silver, not gold, and the depth to which it extends into the wall seems to have been forgotten. The frame projects beyond the wall and appears like the hawsehole of a ship, for its central part, where lies the stone, is dished out—undoubtedly worn that way by the action of millions of lips and hands upon it. The silver casement was made to hold the stone in 1872 (1290 A.D. by the Moslem calendar).

The rationalistic unbeliever supposes this object to be a common aerolite, a remnant of the stone worship which considered it the symbol of power presiding over universal reproduction. There are reasons to believe that it was originally inserted in the wall by Mohammed, for as far back as then it was held to be so sacred that not even he dared destroy it along with the other idols of the *Kaaba*. The relic has fared ill, of that there is no doubt. It has been stolen and broken and has suffered many other accidents. It is believed to have first been white, but the sins of the world are held responsible for turning it black. Moslem historians do not deny it was an object of worship before Islam and it is connected in some legends with the history of other patriarchs before Abraham, beginning as far back as Adam.

The scene in the *Kaaba* square is usually one of the wildest excitement. Many pilgrims are prostrated in adoration while others stand entranced in reverence. The crowd close to the House shove and jostle in hysterical effort to reach the holy curtain, shrieking the *Talbiya* at the top of their lungs while tears streak their dusty faces. They cling to the curtain sobbing as though their hearts were breaking. Some throw their arms toward heaven in attitudes of despairing imploration while attempting to press their wild beating breasts against the sacred shroud. Others fight for the chance to rub their foreheads against the ancient stones. Some are overcome by the high pitch of emotion that possesses the mob and are trampled while others appear ready to faint as they shed floods of tears and pour forth impassioned utterances.

When the newly arrived pilgrim first beholds this scene he is at once entranced. When he finally overcomes his initial fear and awe and is able to move on, he first performs certain ablutions. After this he utters various religious formula and makes two prostration prayers before approaching the Holy of Holies. Slowly he joins in the frenzied mob, and, if fortunate, may eventually reach to kiss the Black Stone. When this is accomplished he has reached the ultimate goal of his entire life. He is held in a state of supreme bliss.

CHAPTER TWENTY-FOUR

The Modern Hajj to Mecca

THE important days of the Hajj are the eighth, ninth and tenth, during which time the essential ceremonies are performed. The eighth day is the traditional date for the great exodus to the village of Mina, three miles beyond the city of Mecca. This exodus is known as *Yaum al Tarwiya*. His Majesty, Abdul Aziz, always attends the central ceremonies during this period. The royal family and entourage of men, women, slaves, children, guards and ministers are transported from the palace to Mina by a fleet of three or four hundred motor vehicles, followed by ten thousand camels.

At Mina the pilgrims spend the night. The plain extends as far as can be seen with tens of thousands of tents. Mina, as well as Arafat, is associated with a tradition about Adam and Eve. It is said that at

Mina, Adam made a wish to see Eve (who was then in Jidda) and that at Arafat he met her.

On the ninth day the multitudes proceed from Mina to the plain of Arafat, for the principal ceremony, the "standing" by *Jabal al Rahma*. Enroute, all who can possibly do so, crowd into the mosque of *Namira* for the midday service conducted by the chief ecclesiastic of Mecca. The mosque stands in the secular strip of valley on the way to the plain of Arafat, which divides that sacred territory from Mecca. With the lack of organization and the vast throngs, this is said to be torture. After the service the pilgrims partake of food then begin the ceremony of the standing at *Jabal al Rahma,* the Mount of Mercy. It is a low granite hummock about 150 feet high and marked by a white pillar. The Faithful must remain here in the broiling sun from two o'clock until sunset, reciting endless prayers prescribed for the occasion.

This ceremony at Arafat is said to be essentially a festival of the camel. At least fifty thousand of the beasts are scattered among the motley crowd, adding their own unceasing lamentations to those of the pilgrims. Although it is called a standing, it is considered better to be mounted on a camel, as the Prophet remained on the back of his she-camel during this ceremony of his farewell pilgrimage. Tradition states that it was also here that God reunited Adam and Eve after being expelled from the Garden of Eden and wandering separately over the earth.

By legend a great wind, believed to be the spirit of God, descends upon the Faithful and though little known outside Moslem circles, all vow that it still happens each year without fail. It is also believed that whenever the number assembled for this occasion is less than 600,000 the balance is made up by angels from heaven. The essence of pilgrimage is to be present for this ceremony, and this part of the *Hajj,* though performed even in a state of insensibility is valid and to die by the wayside is martyrdom, saving all the pains and penalties of the tomb. A visit to the *Kaaba* does not entitle a man to be called *Hajji*, but only by standing at Arafat may he earn this coveted appellation to his name.

When the day is officially ended everyone rushes from Arafat and in the greatest disorder takes the road back toward Mecca to spend the night at Muzdalifa. Many are trampled, litters crushed and camels thrown in the chaotic confusion which is now increased by the presence of hundreds of busses and motor cars.

The tenth day is begun by a performance of another important ceremonial, the obligatory lapidation of the Great Devil at Aqaba. Here there are three pillars called the Great Devil, Middle Devil and First Devil. The pilgrim must select twenty-one bits of granite the size of small beans from the wadi Muhassir and wash them in seven waters. He must approach as close as possible to the Great Devil and cast seven pebbles, one at a time, while reciting with each cast, "In the name of Allah, and Allah is Almighty! In hatred of the Fiend and to his shame I do this!"

This rite is performed in memory of Abraham having driven Satan away with stones when tempted by him to disobey God and refuse to sacrifice Ishmael. Arab legend states that it was Ishmael and not Isaac as recorded in the Bible.

It can be imagined what tremendous mounds of gravel would be assembled over the centuries by the millions of pilgrims but for the reputed miracle resulting in the spontaneous disappearance, by spiritual agency, of each year's contribution before the next execration becomes due.

There are five essential conditions of the *Hajj* proper: 1) to assume *el Ihram;* 2) to stand at Arafat; 3) to stone the Great Devil; 4) to proceed to Mecca and perform *Tawaf;* and 5) to perform *Sa'i*—the running between the hills of As Safa and Al Marwa. After completing these five conditions the pilgrim is released from all the obligations of *el Ihram* and may resume ordinary clothes. If he performs only the first two, leaving the others to another time, he similarly becomes free of all restrictions with the sole exception that intercourse with women is still forbidden until he has fulfilled all five.

The lapidation is performed in the morning, so that many pilgrims are back in Mecca for *Tawif* long before noon. *Tawif,* or circumambulation is the ceremony of circuiting the *Kaaba.* The giant pavement, smooth as glass and hôt as the sun can make it, circles the *Kaaba.* Bare-headed and barefoot the pilgrim joins in the ceremony. It consists of seven rounds of the House, to which the left shoulder is turned, and suggests the idea of perpetual motion with so many persons falling out to be replaced by others. Each spot has its peculiar prayers and at all other times there is a shouting of the *Talbiya* and a complete recital of this peculiar formula of the pilgrim which translates:

> "Here am I! O Allah! here am I!
> No partner hast Thou, here am I!
> Verily the Praise and the Grace are Thine
> and the Kingdom!
> No partner hast Thou, here am I!"

The first three courses of *Tawif* are performed at a brisk trot, the rest at a leisurely pace. The tremendous square is a bedlam of thousands of frenzied devotees, many of them capable of anything in their hysterical states of religious ecstasy, and it is said to be the greatest torture of the entire pilgrimage. The mass of humanity simply exudes heat. Husbands and escorts try to protect their women from the blows and pushes of the frenzied mob of young and aged, blind and halt. The *Multazam* wall (the wall holding the Black Stone) becomes dense with supplicants begging for the forgiveness of God and the remission of their sins.

After completing the seven rounds, other unimportant devotions follow, concluded with a douche at the Zemzem well and with general almsgiving. Each pilgrim is fortified with a small book of ritual prayers and there is great punctiliousness in observing every detail correctly.

Next the ceremony of *Sa'i* is performed, in imitation of Hagar seeking her child. The course is laid out from the Great Mosque to Marwa. At Marwa the pilgrim turns toward Safa. From Safa he begins running between the two points seven times in all—four from Safa to Marwa and three in the reverse direction. It should be performed in a jogging gait, and covers a distance of 2,660 yards in all. This marks the completion of the principal ceremonies of the great pilgrimage, and the men may then be shaved and have their hair cut by one of the army of barbers waiting on the Marwa end of the course.

In the midafternoon the Festival of the Sacrifice, *Id al Adha,* takes place on the plain at Mina (or Muna). It commemorates the story of Abraham when he substituted a ram for Ishmael, father of the later Arabs. This sacrifice is observed simultaneously throughout the entire Moslem world and holds among Moslems the rank that Christmas claims from Christendom. Either a goat, sheep or camel is sacrificed, whichever can be afforded.

The local people make a great deal of money in selling animals, for each pilgrim must kill at least one and for many special reasons he may sacrifice even more. If so, it is usually in expiation of sins, for the Moslem seldom asks God for favors but limits his prayers to thanksgiving and adoration. The distinguishing character of Islam is this attitude toward God. To His Will they submit, Him they constantly praise and glorify and in Him alone do they hope. He is all things:

Loving, Merciful, Just and Good; Awful, Transcendent, Almighty and Supreme. No creature may be compared to Him and to Him alone do they pray. They ask intercession of the prophets and saints but they jealously preserve the distinction between Creator and creature.

In performing the sacrifice the animal is faced toward the *Kaaba* and the knife plunged into its throat with the cry, *"Bismi' allah!"*— "In the name of God." *"Allahu Akbar!"*—"God is omnipotent."

The sacrificial feast follows. Others have written with much critical emotion of the great slaughter that occurs here. This spot has been termed the "Devil's Punchbowl," a "filthy slaughterhouse" and "a threat to all the world." Almost anything that might be said about conditions under the Turks and under the former king, Hussein, is undoubtedly true. Until recently there was a terrible want of cleanliness in the whole affair. Animals were cut up and the uneaten parts left unburied for the vultures and Takarina—the human vultures of Arabia. It must have been a revolting scene, aided by the hot temperature, and justification for the charges of having caused more than one desolating pestilence in the past.

The slaughtering place is now wisely removed to a reasonable distance from the main camps of pilgrims, and since Abdul Aziz there have been no epidemics—a great tribute to him. Furthermore, various Moslem countries now send medical missions to be present throughout the *Hajj.*

After the feasting the great plain becomes a trade mart, resembling an international fair. The multitudes remain for several days during which time they will return to pelt the other two pillars with their fourteen remaining pebbles, as they did the first one. The rite called *Umrah* remains for those who wish to make it and there are various other places of sanctity to be visited, such as the tombs of Hagar and Ishmael in the *Kaaba* square. They will also visit The Place of Abraham. This is a stone upon which Abraham is supposed to have stood while superintending the building (or rebuilding) of the *Kaaba*.

The last ceremony performed is the *Tawif el Widaa,* or Circumambulation of Farewell. This is a very sad occasion. After circling the House the pilgrim approaches to kiss the Black Stone again with the salutation, "In the name of God; and God is Great." Next he kisses the threshold of the door and when possible presses his face and palpitating bosom against the wall. While clinging to the curtain he sobs and groans in sublime moments of ecstasy. He recites religious formula and praises the Prophet until finally backing away with many salutations and prostrations. On reaching the Gate of Farewell he gives a long parting glance to *Beit Allah,* for he may never see it again. Then, as the crowds push him on, he slowly turns his ecstatic face homeward.

Although the pilgrimage to Mecca is obligatory, the one to Medina, called the *Ziyarat,* is not; but it is considered meritorious. Many make the trip either before or after visiting Mecca, as the tomb of the Prophet is there and also his mosque. Medina too is holy and forbidden to unbelievers. The Place of the Tomb has four large gates that are carefully locked and guarded by eunuchs, probably because Islam forbids pilgrimages to or adoration of tombs. The pilgrim goes to Medina because next to Mecca it figured most prominently in the life of Mohammed. One of the Prophet's last utterances before he died was, "Oh Lord, let not my tomb be ever an object of worship."

Four graves are within the Place of the Tomb, those of Mohammed; Abu Bekr, a father-in-law; Omar, founder of the imperial power of Islam; and Fatima, the Prophet's beloved daughter.

After the principal days of the *Hajj* were over, we watched as endless streams of exhausted pilgrims began to wander back into Jidda to take ship. Many became stranded and were either transported by their respective governments or else remained until money could be earned for their return needs. The men could now wear a green band in their turbans and bear the coveted title *Hajji*. All, however, were cleansed from the sins of the past and all might carry the peace of Allah in their hearts for having obeyed the words of the Prophet and fulfilled their religious duty.

When the last had finally departed, perhaps a month or two later, Jidda gradually settled back into its lassitude and indolent ways. Prices came down and the riyal fell to its normal value. Again a hushed, furtive atmosphere returned to inhabit the town; an atmosphere as of something unhealthy left behind, making it seem again as lifeless as a city of the dead.

CHAPTER TWENTY-FIVE

Famous Converts to Islam

No ONE in our times ever understood the Arabs better than the late Lawrence of Arabia, their culture and mental processes; nor has there been anyone more sympathetic to them. Yet he confessed that the effort of his years of living and dressing as an Arab and imitating their mental foundation, quitted him of his English self and permitted him to see the West and its conventions—destroyed for him in the process —with new eyes. After his singular experience he maintained that he could not sincerely take on the Arab skin either; it being a pretense and affectation only, and that man was easily made an infidel but hardly might he be converted to another faith. Lawrence said he had dropped one form and had not been able to take on the other, but could see things through the veils at once of two customs, two educations and two environments—a situation that he termed as near to madness. This caused him to pray that men would not, for love of glamor and strangeness, barter their souls and prostitute themselves and their talents in serving another race.

It must be a strange experience to forsake one's own culture for that of another race, but even stranger to also adopt their philosophy and religion. Yet two men in our midst appeared to have successfully performed the transition, despite the experience and observations of the esteemed Lawrence.

One of these Christian converts to Islam was an amiable but rather doddering Dutchman, well known throughout the East as Arthur Van der Poll. Arthur was one of the oldest residents of Jidda, having gone there over forty years ago and survived—this fact alone qualifying him for fame. His wife and family lived in Europe where he returned every few years to see them.

Arthur originally went to Jidda to represent a Dutch commercial firm, but soon formed his own trading company which he has managed successfully since. Arthur never said whether he found it expedient in those early days to become a Moslem in the pursuit of his interests or was truly a convert. However, it was not for one to judge. The fact remains that he was accepted as a convert and to all appearances was a devout one. He attended the *Hajj* each year, carried his beads and prayed the prescribed number of times each day.

Arthur had worn Arab dress for so many years, he would have looked odd in any other costume. The voluminous folds of his flowing white robes canopied a substantial bulk, shod in Arab sandals and cowled in a white-cotton *qhotra*. He never wore headropes but draped the long ends of the *qhotra* about his neck in peasant fashion. Beneath bushy gray eyebrows peered wide blue eyes and from the point of his chin sprouted a belligerent goatee. The excited whisper of his animated voice, added to the startled expression of his eyes, produced the impression that Arthur was perpetually surprised. He frequently called to impart choice bits of local gossip in such awed intensity as to make him stutter, causing the most unimportant matters to assume the quality of scandal.

The gazelle was intrigued with Arthur because he looked like an Arab but did not smell like one—a puzzling situation. Arthur rushed from Fred's office one day into mine. "Your gazelle just bit my finger!" he exclaimed in the same amazed tone of voice he would have employed to say, "Your gazelle just spoke to me in Arabic!"

As Donald only had teeth in the back of his lower jaw, I replied, "Well, Arthur, what was your finger doing down his throat?" This implied that he could sue me if he liked, but surely Donald had a right to bite whatever might be thrust down his throat.

Another local personality was the renowned Harry St. John B. Philby, British mentor and confidant of Abdul Aziz. He was the only other Christian convert to the Moslem faith.

In 1916 England needed every ally she could find. Philby was then political officer on the civil commissioners staff in Baghdad. Although Abdul Aziz was then in control of only central Arabia, he could nevertheless be of value to the British in the struggle of power between themselves and the Germans over the Persian Gulf. Philby was sent on a mission, along with Lord Belhaven, to secure the king's alliance, and he has remained in Arabia ever since.

Philby embraced Islam shortly after becoming associated with the king. Since then he not only finds time to handle his business of representing British commercial interests, but also to write magnificent books on the Middle East and to furnish the king with advice and counsel. Philby is well known as an accomplished author, a learned scholar, traveler and explorer, and is considered the outstanding authority on Saudi Arabia, the Yemen and the Hadhramaut. He has even explored the unmapped quarters of the *Rhubl el Khali* in southeastern Arabia, a place where few men ever have been.

Philby enjoys a position of confidence and friendship at the palace never accorded any other outsider. Indeed his activities and influence have caused him to be referred to, and with some justification, as "the unsung Lawrence of Arabia." However, around the time of my assignment to Arabia, he fell out of favor with the British and also became *persona non grata* with the Saudis. All of his property was confiscated and he was forbidden ever to enter the country again. Apparently his position in Arabia got the better of his common sense and he abused his privileges. The king, however, is well known for his forgiving nature and generous ways, and whatever the difficulty, it was not long before Philby was back in Arabia and settled again in his old position.

Philby now maintains a house in Jidda and one in Mecca—a unique privilege. In heavy dark beard and Arab robes, he looks exactly like one of the Smith Brothers (of cough-drop fame) wearing a shawl.

To anyone but a close friend, Philby is studiously indifferent and seems wrapped in an unapproachable cloak of conscious self-importance. Yet, quietly unobtrusive behind the familiar scenes of Riyadh and Mecca, he is credited for having had much to do with the king's rise to his present prominence of power and prestige in the Arab world.

PART V

CHAPTER TWENTY-SIX

The Comforting Night

THE hour of sunset was by habit the time for a general exodus from the city. Just when the sinking sun turned the sea into burnished gold and the dull Hijaz hills into soft pastel colors, groups of Moslems wandered beyond the city wall to recite their evening prayers. Unbelievers, like Donald and myself, enjoyed a run in the desert at this, the most pleasant time of day.

As we prepared to leave Beit Najib a sedan car sometimes drew to the side door of a house nearby to whisk the wives of Sheikh Yusuf off toward Mecca for the one breath of freedom they might sometimes enjoy. We caught only a fleeting glimpse of black-gowned and well-veiled female figures as they dashed from the doorway to the waiting car. Even the car was heavily veiled inside so that no prying masculine eye might violate their privacy.

Donald and I rode in an open jeep. The rough and dusty thorough-fare followed the wall until finding the Mecca Gate, and at this hour contained only men and goats. The goats possessed a philosophy quite different from men in regard to traffic. They sensibly scattered; but any sleepwalking Somali or Takruni had to be approached with caution, loud blasts of the horn and preparation for any erratic action. He was very apt to flush like a frightened rabbit just at the moment of passing. Instead of moving away from the vehicle, he invariably gathered up his skirts and dashed in wild abandon directly into its path in what seemed to be a frenzied attempt to test the will of God and the durability of his body, if not that of the jeep. He was philo-sophical about it in his way, for whatever happened, must happen— *insha' Allah!*

The one hard-surfaced road ran from Jidda to Mecca, forty-six miles inland. Only recently had it become possible for non-Moslems to go outside the city without permission, but I quite naturally viewed this freedom elastically and often drove within a few miles of the for-bidden area. An Arab friend often invited me to accompany him all the way into the city, and knowing of his propensities as well as the frequency of his trips only whetted my curiosity about this most mys-terious city. Since it is believed that until recently Mecca was perhaps the most evil and licentious in the world, I often promised to accom-pany him and find out. Several times I followed in the jeep until reaching the police block, but aware that the fanatical people would tear apart any intruder who got beyond the police, I always recalled my fondness for life and my diplomatic responsibilities and sensibly retreated.

I often took the gazelle in that direction for his evening exercise. When we reached an area of flat shingle I turned off the road and permitted him the pleasure of bounding across its hard surface. He was fond of racing the jeep providing I did not exceed forty miles an hour. For such a pace he seemed to throw himself into high gear, bouncing as though made of spring steel. His hoofs seemed hardly to touch the sand before he bounced into the air again, each time covering a distance of ten feet or more.

Although Donald's form was good to see, his speed and endurance was short lived. When his tongue hung from his panting open mouth, I slowed down and then stopped to praise and pet his heaving sides. He was content for awhile to accept this expected attention before racing off again in erratic spurts of speed. When whistled for he returned in the greatest possible haste, pretending to run me down but skidding to a halt in my arms.

We sometimes drove on beyond the tiny oasis of Wadi Fatima where the barren landscape always astonished me. The very rocks themselves were turned a greasy black by the sun's heat. Such a land was not lovely, yet its silent, austere grandeur held a compelling attraction. Before learning to know the desert, I had often wondered why the Bedou wanted to live there and how they could extract a living from such a wilderness of sand and baked mountains. Such a place seemed incapable of supporting any life whatever, but goats and camels lived there and their masters with them. There existed a profound partnership between them, the men contributing leadership and protection and the animals contributing a capacity for survival that could not be defeated. They found enough sustenance among the thorn scrub and bare rocks to maintain themselves and their masters with them.

When we turned back and again passed through the small oasis I realized how beautiful a wadi can be. Its little shade and greenness brought joy to one's heart and I agreed with the Arabs that "heaven is simply a perfect oasis."

The spring water of the wadi was channeled in and out among the trees and on into little fields of emerald green *dukhn* (millet). It could be diverted here and there by stopping one channel with a little soil and opening another, so that it was parceled out to the maximum extent. The trees were date palms, for wherever water is found they always appear with their feathery tops and welcome shade. Their fruit, plus the meat and milk supplied by goats, provides enough for the Bedouins' meager needs. The date palm is considered the outward and visible sign of a near and spiritual benevolence because where palms grow there is water, and water is the Grace of Allah, the gift of life to man.

Beside the Mecca road, the only other direction in which we could drive was northward, along the uninhabited coast toward Medina. About twenty miles north of Jidda there was a spot where a deep sea-inlet cut sharply into the desert. The inlet was perhaps a mile wide and extended only several miles into the desert as if unable to advance further into the consuming heat and thirsty sand. We named this inlet "the creek" and often swam there.

The creek was doubtless caused ages ago by an upheaval of land formerly under the sea. The coastal plain was still covered with sea-shells, and hard coral could be found at any point beneath the sands. It was no more than a large crack or fault in the earth's surface into which the sea had found its way. A white coral shelf extended from the shore of the creek, gradually deepening to perhaps twenty feet, then suddenly dropping off into bottomless dark blue water.

About one hundred yards from shore and near the edge of the shelf, we built a float from petrol drums and wooden planks. It was the only "safe" spot we had found, but, even so, there remained the constant threat of sharks, barracuda, men-of-war and a great variety of poisonous fish and sea snakes, sea urchins and poison coral.

The bites of poisonous fish found in the warm waters of the Red

Sea are always painful and sometimes fatal. These troublesome creatures hide in rocks and coral tangles, blending harmoniously with their surroundings while awaiting the chance to attack whatever might interest them. The fishermen who wade the lagoons with weighted throw-nets, sing and beat the water with long sticks to frighten them away.

The barracuda of the Red Sea will attack any moving object and can inflict severe wounds, but the shark can remove a limb without even trying. I feared the man-of-war more than any other danger for I had seen a man paralyzed in the water from only a brush of the invisible tentacles. The octopus was harmless unless one was foolish enough to pick him up, as I once did. I learned to my grief that he was equipped with a long and sharp incisor tooth. I had no sooner picked up the threshing creature than he pierced the palm of my hand with this tooth, causing me to fling him down in a great hurry.

One might wonder why we were so foolhardy as to swim at all, but the light coral and clear water made it possible to keep an eye open for these dangers. Limited recreation made us attempt any sport that promised some diversion or excitement.

Donald always went along to the creek and roamed the desert to his heart's content. If he became lonesome on shore, he waded into the water with casual self-assurance and swam out to join us on the raft. He looked like a small sea monster in the water, as only his head and large ears, supported by a long neck, were visible. The effect was quite startling if he appeared in our midst suddenly and without warning.

We sometimes swam in the creek at night. The moon was full and we had planned a desert party at the time General Sir Harold Alexander paid a sudden visit to Jidda. The British minister gave an unexpected soiree for him on the residency roof and we were obliged to attend.

The night was hot and humid as usual, and the oppressive air completely motionless. Despite the fact that everyone dressed informally with only white linens, open shirts and cummerbunds, our light clothes were dripping wet and crumpled even before making an appearance. The six women summoned for the occasion were too enervated by the enduring heat to dance. They sat gasping like fish out of water, highball in one hand and fan in the other. The only point in the evening's favor was the bright moon. It cast sufficient light to read by, making long dark shadows from the buildings at hand and causing us to long for the creek.

After a few cooling drinks and regardless of the presence of such other august guests as Admiral Sir Andrew Cunningham and Field Marshall Sir Alan Brooke, Fred and I decided we could stand the heat no longer. No one else felt up to such recklessness, but we considered the possibility of a swim more enticing than the minister's good Scotch and the necessity for polite behavior.

The trail to the creek followed uncertainly along the seacoast. Our headlights often caught small gray-white jerboas in their glare. We slowed down or turned aside to avoid injuring them, and on stopping found them to be sociable and friendly, hopping about on their tiny hind legs without fear, their beady black eyes reflecting consuming curiosity in our presence.

We found the water to be warm but it felt refreshing, and swimming in it, uninhibited as nature produced us, was like bathing in liquid moonlight. The brilliance of the moon transformed the bleak landscape into a place of unnatural beauty. It imparted a luminous quality to the water, making it possible to see clearly every detail of the coral bottom to the limit where it dropped off into a dark ribbon of depthless blue. When Fred plunged from the raft, streaks of bubbly light followed him in phosphorescent trails like a meteor flushing the sky.

We were both in the water when a school of tremendous brown shapes suddenly broke the surface close by, splashing madly and terrifying us for a moment. We thought them sharks and by sheer reflex action were quickly out of the water and onto the raft. Only then did we realize that they were porpoises. We laughed in relief but considered it our cue to return to safer pastimes.

We sped back across the moonlit plain, refreshed and glad once more that to the desert had been given the cooling, comforting night.

CHAPTER TWENTY-SEVEN

It Is Written

ALTHOUGH the Arab race once gave great physicians to the world, their present ideas on the art of healing are often barbarous. The practices among the low-caste Somali, Takruni and Arab dockworkers are particularly appalling. They believe the best treatment for a bruise is cautery with a hot iron and it is not uncommon to see them beat a mashed foot with a switch or stick to drive out the pain. The cure for rheumatism is puncture by a red-hot needle. Open cuts or wounds are often salved with animal dung and flowing wounds checked by dust from the street. The remedy is usually more serious than the original injury.

The fishermen contract various afflictions. Scurvy spots on their skin, caused by salt burns or improper diet, are rubbed with chewed tobacco. Tropical ulcerations are common and often spread to become large and obstinate pustulations. Various treatments are followed, from searing with hot irons to the wearing of Koranic amulets.

Most of the more barbarous customs are practiced by the black races from Africa and have been carried by them to Arabia. The driving out of devils occurs there as it does among the most uncivilized tribes in other lands. The victim seems to be placed into a hypnotic state by long measured chanting and then a few red-hot cinders are placed in his mouth. These he chews and swallows with no apparent pain or aftereffects but promptly enters into a deep sleep. On waking he is pronounced free of his evil spirits.

Surprisingly little malaria exists in Arabia as a whole. There remains the constant threat of it however, as with sand-fly fever, typhus, plague, smallpox, yellow fever and other tropical diseases. We were inoculated for most of them but it was practically impossible to prevent dysentery and respiratory ailments. There was one case of typhoid during my residence there and a number of other strange, undiagnosed cases among the European colony.

After dysentery, prickly heat remains the most painful cross for the white man to bear. The effect of the hot and humid climate on the skin can be easily imagined when its action on metals and leather was so apparent. Leather articles rot quickly and grow thick coats of mildew even though wrapped carefully and kept in trunks. My jeep required an oil or kerosene bath as often as I needed soap and water, and even then rusted away. My typewriter had to be bathed in kerosene each week in the hope that it would last as long as I might.

The plague of Arabia and the greatest carrier of disease is the common fly. When to this situation is added the fatalistic Arab philosophy, it is astonishing that life has survived there for so many thousands of years. I never quite succeeded in overcoming my horror at seeing the

Takruni babies with their eyes solidly plastered by flies and, as in Egypt, I marveled that neither the mothers nor the children ever bothered to brush them away.

The Saudi government operated a small and inadequate hospital in Jidda. It was understaffed and generally lacking in everything that constituted a hospital and consequently rendered a most limited service to the Arabs for whom it was run. In cases of serious illness among the Europeans it was necessary to move them to the British hospital in the Anglo-Egyptian Sudan or else to Cairo or Beirut where adequate medical attention was available.

With the building of the oil company hospital at Dhahran, it became possible for Americans to receive medical care without leaving Arabia, but it was often easier to fly to Cairo than to obtain a ride across the desert to Dhahran.

Very little disease was apparent among the Saudi Arabs except trachoma and eye troubles of every kind. However, surveys have shown them to be greatly afflicted with all kinds of pulmonary and venereal diseases also. Tuberculosis and smallpox with occasional epidemics of dengue are the worst scourges of the land. Philby states that he obtained figures covering a period of three months from the government clinic at Riyadh and he claims that these figures showed only approximately five percent of the population in the Najd to be suffering from syphilis. However, with the influx of pilgrims on the Red Sea side, the picture was quite different. The records of an experimental clinic established in Jidda for a short time by our own government showed seventy-five percent of the patients examined to be suffering from both tuberculosis and syphilis. By comparison, however, the native Saudi population in general are not nearly so diseased, nor as subject to the great variety of diseases, as the pilgrims who go there or as the natives of more congested countries such as Egypt.

Approximately seventy percent of the infants succumb within their first year and those who survive the first few years of their lives have a fair chance of reaching maturity. Having reached maturity they seem to build up enough resistance to carry them into quite old age. The Saudi Arab may not look strong and may be infected with several diseases and he is, of course, undernourished and anemic; but over centuries of rigorous existence he has developed such stamina and immunity that he is able to continue living under the most severe conditions and on a quantity of sustenance that would be fatal to a less inured race. Thirst and hunger are the constant companions of the Bedouin, but they are so accustomed to long periods of privations that it affects them as little as it does their enduring camels.

As part of our aid program, the health of the population was a major consideration. Medical supplies and hospital equipment were as important as foodstuffs and textiles. Although we imported quantities of medicines and equipment for use in the government hospitals in Jidda and Riyadh, there remained the problem of doctors and nurses to staff these wholly inadequate dispensaries. It has been part of Ibn Saud's plan to establish wider public health facilities for his people and to staff them with Moslem doctors from other countries. Our initial aid has helped him in this direction and has been greatly augmented by the assistance of Aramco. All Aramco Arab employees and their families now receive medical attention at hospitals and health centers established at Ras Tanura, Dhahran, Ras Misha'ab and Abqaiq. This service is gradually spreading to a great many thousands of Saudis and will in time have considerable effect on the health of the nation as a whole.

Much of the oil company's medical work is now of a preventive nature in the form of vaccinations and immunizations against certain diseases. On a more imposing scale are their efforts to control the spread of disease transmitted by insects and rodents and those transferred through food, water, wastes or human carriers. Aramco doctors are waging a war against flies and mosquitoes and against unsanitary practices which spread disease.

The greatest task to be accomplished is one of education, as most of the Arabs' ills are caused through malnutrition, lack of sanitation and sheer ignorance. Unfortunately their ascetic religion can be blamed for many of their afflictions.

In founding Islam, the Prophet very intelligently kept in mind the austerity of the climate, the poverty of the desert and the rigorous demands that life makes upon the Arabs' faith and powers of endurance. He created a religion that is so ideally compatible with these conditions as to easily make Allah the chief refuge. In this refuge the ignorant and unenlightened exercise an excessive fatalism or blind faith in the Will of God, and this becomes the destructive force in the religion. If an infant dies through neglect or disregard of simple hygienic principles, the parents' casual attitude is expressed in *"insha' Allah"* ("As God wills"), or *maktoub* ("It is written"). It seems beyond their grasp to understand that a few ordinary precautions on their part would have changed "the Will of God" and saved the infant's life.

In every detail of the Arabs' daily life too much is left to God's will. As has been said before, it is a wonderful attitude within reasonable limits, but in Arabia, as in other countries, Providence is severely overworked.

CHAPTER TWENTY-EIGHT

The Land of Sheba

ON AN April morning the United States destroyer *Ernest G. Small* sailed from Jidda and headed south for the Kingdom of Yemen, the Land of Sheba. Its mission was an historic one. Aboard were our minister, Colonel Eddy, and his staff of advisors including Fred. This was Fred's great adventure, for like everyone who has ever heard of the Yemen, he had long been fascinated by that little known and least explored of independent Arab States. As an Arabic student he had studied the Yemen's ancient civilization and the opportunity to at last go there was like the realization of a dream.

Although it was Fred's adventure, the great interest of the Yemen itself, as well as the fact that it is an integral part of the picture of Arabia, perhaps justifies my including a few of the little known but interesting facts concerning this remote section of Arabia.

The Kingdom of Yemen is situated in the southwestern end of the Arabian Peninsula and today covers only 75,000 square miles of territory, a very small part of this tremendous land area. It is the most populated section of Arabia, containing an estimated three to four million inhabitants. The soil of the Tihama, or coastal plain is sparsely cultivated for want of irrigation but the interior mountains, which rise to nearly 11,000 feet, catch considerable rainfall and the exceedingly fertile valleys and plateaus abound in grain, fruit and the world-famous Mocha coffee. The green terraced fields rise in geometric patterns from the low valleys far up the slopes of towering mountains.

The Yemen has never been exposed to Western influence and remains in many respects as it was in the days of its once celebrated ruler, the Queen of Sheba. The glory and accomplishments of that illustrious era have vanished but there still exists many reminders of the splendor of the civilizations that once flourished there.

The ruins of tremendous dams and waterworks can still be seen today. Marib, the fabulous capital of old, lies crumbling in the shifting sands that cover large areas once green and abundant. The great dam that burst in the fifth century A.D. was never rebuilt, so the once fertile fields of Marib have been reclaimed by the desert and the flourishing centers of population have long since disappeared. To further the Yemen's decline, the development of commerce through the Red Sea by-passed the old overland trade routes, thus cutting off an important source of Yemeni wealth.

The early loss of independence also contributed to the Yemen's downfall through the ages. The Minaean Kingdom, the earliest recorded government, was overthrown by those great Egyptian conquerors, Thothmes II and Thothmes III in 1600 B.C., followed by varying degrees of Roman and Ethiopian subjugation and control. In 626

A.D. the Prophet Mohammed dispatched his envoys to carry the creed of Islam to adjoining nations and his nephew, Ali, converted the Yemen to Islam, after which it was ruled by governors appointed by the caliphs.

The Turks first established themselves in the sixteenth century but later lost control of the highlands. Mohammed Ali of Egypt reoccupied the coast in 1819 and finally in 1872 Ottoman power was again established over the entire country. After many serious revolts a degree of autonomy was granted the country, but not until the close of World War I was their rule finally overthrown and complete independence attained.

The Imam, or king, at the time of the Eddy Mission was El-Mutuwakel Al-Allah Yahya bin Mohammed Hamidudin. His dynasty dated from the tenth century and he began his rule in 1902 under the Turks. After gaining independence in 1918 the country enjoyed a period of peace until 1934 when the Imam had some territorial difficulties with Abdul Aziz over the province of Asir. After a series of border clashes the Saudis invaded the Yemen and took San'a, the capital. Then, feeling that the Yemenis had been taught a lesson, they withdrew and left the country entirely independent. The Lord of Arabia offered a most generous peace treaty and did not annex any territory to which Yemen had just claim. The treaty pledged the signatories to submit further disputes to arbitration, to refrain from aiding insurrections in the others' territory and to promote the unity of the Arab nations.

Both its geographical position and the old autocratic Yahya are responsible for the present-day backwardness of a land which the Romans called *Arabia Felix* or Happy Arabia.

The American destroyer sailed from Jidda, south through the Red Sea, stopping at the Cameron Islands before putting the mission ashore at Hodeida, the seaport for San'a. From Hodeida they traveled overland by jeep, through the tortuous, lofty mountains and deep valleys until reaching the capital high in the interior. Fred said that entering San'a was like leaving the twentieth century and turning far back among the faded pages of history. Its ancient palaces, walls and fortifications were of another, bygone age.

Relations between the United States and Yemen had always in the past been conducted on an informal basis through the consulate at Aden. The purpose of the Eddy Mission was to formally recognize the independence of Yemen, at the Imam's request, and to negotiate a treaty of friendship and commerce.

Full details of the negotiations held with the Imam and his ministers have not yet been made public but the mission met with many difficulties and only through the patience, tact and ingenuity of Colonel Eddy was a treaty ever concluded. It remains for this accomplished diplomat to add a thrilling chapter to the modern *Arabian Nights* by someday recording the entire story of his historic visit.

In brief, the difficulties encountered were caused not only by the mistrust and suspicions existing in the Imam's court but chiefly by the intrigue and rivalries among his ten sons. The family seemed always at war and even then several of the princes were incarcerated in dungeons. The Crown Prince, Seif * el Islam Ahmed, expected to win the throne at the death of his aged father but he was opposed by the rivalry of his brothers—Hussein, who nominally administered the government, and Ibrahim.

One of the few enlightened and honest men in the court was a Turk named Qadi Raghib Bey. He had remained in the Yemen since World War I to act for the king as his minister of foreign affairs and had served loyally and faithfully for many long years. His shrewdness in the conduct of foreign affairs was undoubtedly responsible for the

---

* Seif el Islam means "Sword of Islam" and is used by all the king's sons.

Imam's political power.

At one critical point in the negotiations Raghib Bey, in vexation and anger at court obstructionism, nearly lost control of his head—in more than one sense. The king was seated upon a raised *roshan,* dressed in richly brocaded robes, stockinged feet and a large silk turban. He was short and fat and droll-looking, his full white beard completing the suggestion of a little Santa Claus. Royal guards stood on either side the "throne" and the American mission and court advisors all sat about the audience chamber on somewhat lower seats.

Raghib Bey indignantly arose to support the American position and to sharply censure the palace intriguers whose actions reflected upon his own integrity. He addressed the Imam without permission, reminding him of his years of service and devotion. At this dramatic point the king's bodyguard advanced with drawn daggers upon Raghib Bey and stood poised, awaiting a signal to slay him. The tensed assembly held its breath, no longer aware of the year.

Raghib Bey had the courage to continue, feeling his time had come anyway. He denounced the plotters, the king's sons, and concluded by offering his resignation. Only then did the Imam finally wave the guards aside. With his imperceptible gesture the daggers were lowered and the anxious audience relaxed and began to breathe again. Raghib Bey retired intact but the Americans held much concern for his safety. Later, when the mission was ready to depart from San'a, Colonel Eddy made several diplomatic attempts to take Raghib Bey with him but this permission was not granted.

After many days of trying delay and patient waiting, while the court continued to intrigue among themselves, Colonel Eddy submitted an ultimatum. A treaty was then promptly signed, the first ever to be concluded between the United States and the Yemen. The mission gladly took its departure, wondering what might be the eventual outcome of this modern drama laid in ancient Yemen.

We did not have long to wait. Early in 1948 a buzz of rumors emerged from Yemen that as usual were veiled in mystery and have yet to receive any official confirmation. This much is definitely known, however. The old man, Imam Yahya, was murdered while riding a donkey on his way to the mosque. Two or three of his sons and some of his key advisors were also slaughtered. Abdullah el Wazir, a wealthy merchant, seized the throne and for a short time called himself Imam while Prince Ibrahim acted as premier of a so-called constitutional government. A story circulated that the old Imam had expected such a happening and had buried forty million dollars worth of his immense treasure in the desert. The slaves, it was naturally said, were then killed to keep the hiding place secret.

The United Nations dispatched a delegation to Arabia to determine the true facts of the situation in Yemen. They only reached Riyadh, however, and were never permitted to enter Yemen. Shortly after this, Prince Ahmed, heir by his father's choice, captured San'a and ousted Abdullah el Wazir, proclaiming himself the new Imam. Prince Abdullah was imprisoned and has since been reported dead. No mention has been made of the fate of Prince Ibrahim nor of the loyal subject Qadi Raghib Bey. The Arab League, to which Yemen belongs, reported civil war raging at the time Imam Yahya was murdered and requested foreign nations to keep their hands off Yemen's private affairs.

CHAPTER TWENTY-NINE

The Flower of Paradise

ALTHOUGH the Arabic word *"yemin"* means "right-hand," the Arabic root "ymn" means "prosperity and happiness" and one may suppose that this root is the origin of the name.

Yemen's ancient civilization, fame and wealth were first described by the early historians and geographers, Strabo and Pliny. It is still possible to distinguish the three principal racial types mentioned by the third-century (B.C.) historian, Eratosthenes. Strabo quotes him as saying that southern Arabia was inhabited by the Sabaeans in the extreme west, the Katabanians in the center and the people of the Hadhramaut in the east. The Sabaeans and Hadhramis are of very great antiquity and are mentioned in the Book of Genesis.

The present-day Yemenis are believed to be descendants of the

Sabaeans. The average Yemeni is of medium height with an olive complexion and small features, his head either shaved clean or his straight black hair worn very short. The costumes of these southern Arabians are different from those further north. The *qhotra, agal* and *mishlah* of Saudi Arabia are almost unknown, the popular garment being a simple skirt or sarong that is draped about the hips so that it falls into pleats in front with the top deftly rolled so that it remains in place. This *futa,* as it is called, can be worn in two different lengths, either to the knees or to the ankles and is a comfortable garment for such a climate.

Men of the more civilized tribes and all city dwellers wear jackets with sleeves and turbans, but the primitive tribes wear only the *futa* with no clothing on the upper part of their bodies. The primitive tribes usually wear their hair long and bound into a bun held by an ornament, and to withstand the rigors of heat and cold rub sesame oil on their heads and bodies. Some tribes add a coating of indigo which they seem to like so well it is used also in dyeing their garments and turbans. To the turban is often added a sprig of sweet herbs or rak, serving as a toothpick at odd moments as well as an ornament. Beards are rare among the southern tribesmen, most of whom carry a pair of small tweezers with which to remove hairs as they appear. The practice of using kohl to beautify the eyes is more common in Yemen than elsewhere. All go barefoot except those of the hill country who wear a rough sandal made from goat hide. The sandals worn by the city dwellers of Hodeida, Mocha and San'a are most unique, intricately decorated with gold thread and designs in small strips of red, green and yellow leather.

Regardless of the variety of clothes and customs, all tribesmen wear a dagger belt and many carry rifles as well. The daggers are curved and pointed and their scabbards are made of filigreed silver, the most ornate, made by the San'a Jews, being washed in gold and set with cornelians or other semiprecious stones. Here, too, the Arabs wear Koranic amulets about their necks or arms.

One of the most interesting tribes are the *Humumis* who inhabit an area to the southeast, near the Hadhramaut. This extensive, warlike tribe are a race of prognathous dwarfs; that is, their lower jaws extend beyond the upper part of their faces, similar to apes. They are small, cunning men, apparently immune to civilizing influences and seem to be a neolithic survival.

Another interesting race are the *Aulaqis* and their related tribes who also live in the southeast, although they may be seen in other parts of the Yemen too. All agree that they are handsome men of magnificent physiques, tall, full-hipped and all having the common feature of large dark eyes and hawklike noses. Their skin is brick-red in color, an oddity produced by the natural pigmentation of their blood. The men often wear a flower in their jet-black hair which is cut in long bobs level with their shoulders. Their Arabic is oddly softened in pronunciation but spoken in a curious high-pitched staccato manner. One of the most surprising facts regarding this strange race is that they are the hardiest and most warlike of all the Arabian peoples.

Unlike Saudi Arabia where there are no Jews and where Jews are not even permitted to enter, many are found in Yemen. They have been there since the beginning of time and are the skilled craftsmen. Much could be written about them. Their persons are sacrosanct or inviolable, and wherever they live it is in complete harmony with their Moslem neighbors. They dress as the Arabs and in places where it is done, they too dye their bodies indigo. Side curls and the absence of arms are the Yemeni Jew's badge of immunity and his only distinguishing feature.

The mode of life varies as greatly as do the ethnic types, but nomadism does not exist here as in other parts of Arabia. The forms of habitation vary from the communities of tremendous villas and palaces to the solitary family living in a mud hut perched atop some remote mountain peak. Houses and villages are not confined to the valleys and plains but are more often built on wild hill tops or perched on apparently inaccessible heights for protection. These towered houses are built strong and substantially of stone and brick and are called *dars*. They are often a complex of fortifications, reminiscent of medieval European architecture and were originally built for defense, with gun slots and holes for dropping stones on unwelcome visitors.

The larger villages consist of a group of *dars,* the largest occupied by the ruling tribesman, overlooking lower ones with the mud huts of the cultivators sprawled at their base, on the edge of sheer cliffs. The most pretentious *dars* might be six or eight stories high, like the houses in San'a, and, like them, boast a high standard of comfort. They have been referred to as the ancient progenitor of the modern skyscraper.

Backwardness, illiteracy and addiction to *qat* seem to be the chief characteristics of the present-day Yemenis. They are strongly addicted to chewing the astringent leaves of a shrub natural to the country. The few visitors claim the curse of the country is the excessive use of this bitter leaf and that the habit is a serious social evil, undermining the mental and physical health of the population; the foe of thrift and industry.

It is little known to the rest of the world and scientific books are almost silent on the subject, yet no Yemeni Arab passes a day if he can help it without the aid of at least a few leaves of the precious plant. It is believed to have been introduced from Ethiopia about 1430, but the Arabs say it has always been, for Allah gave it to them to make them forget labor and pain.

In Yemeni towns and villages everyone dissappears from noontime until the late afternoon. The rich men retire to the *mabraz* in the top of their homes to smoke the *hubbuk* (water pipe) or to chew *qat*. These rooms of the upper class are furnished with Oriental luxury but the less wealthy must patronize a public *mabraz*. In some towns the custom is also followed in the evenings after sunset prayers but in Hodeida only the lower classes, servants and laborers chew *qat* before four in the afternoon, the hour when all business ceases there. In the delightfully cool climate of San'a there is no interruption of business for *qat* chewing.

The statements of Turkish doctors in the Yemen and the few authorities on the subject all agree on the essential facts regarding *qat*. They state that even the poorest classes indulge in the habit, the degree of addiction being in proportion to the amount procurable. The leaves and tender twigs are chewed for their exhilarant properties, it being a stimulant with most and with others a sedative. At first there is a pleasant sensation of intellectual ability and it is said that parties of *qat*-eaters will sit up all night discussing everything and anything.

As with alcohol, *qat* is an acquired taste. Unlike alcohol, however, it contains no demon. The Arab calls it the "flower of paradise," the poor man's happiness, the strength of the weak and the inspiration of the mean-spirited. Without it he is apathetic, evasive and dull. Just what the toxic effect is on the human system has never been ascertained. As a stimulant it is said to have a lively and immediate effect upon the brain and nerve cells, the gloomiest man becoming cheerful under its influence and the most enervated, active. By and by the habitué finds himself incapable of clear and consecutive thought without the herb and attains an imbecilic expression. The teeth become much affected, permanently discolored and loose as the gums become flaccid. By this time the victim is incapable of intelligent thought or efficient work by any accidental deprivation.

In cases of slight addiction the only marked failing is that of memory and men who enjoy *qat* but can only get it in small quantities and at long intervals are very little affected. It always produces, however, a certain mental fuzziness even after a short indulgence, the natural reaction after a strong nervous stimulant.

Those who indulge in *qat* admit its bad effects but claim they cannot do without it. *Qat* permeates every class that can afford it and many that cannot and although it takes the place with Arabs of alcohol, they regard the suggestion that it would be condemned by the Prophet as a moot point since the leaf was unknown in his time.

Some doctors state that constant use and overindulgence appear to finally sap one's energies and to induce constipation, insomnia and eventually impotency. Erotic attachments were found to be common among the ruling class in Yemen and it may be a matter for speculation whether the pernicious leaf has anything to do with the matter.

Catha edulis is the plant's botanical name and the word (*qat, kat* or *khat*) is said to be derived from the Arabic word *kut,* meaning sustenance or reviving principle. It refers to the most salient property of the plant—that of exalting the spirits and supporting bodily strength. A French writer has said, *"La destinèe des nations dépend de la manière dont elles se nourrissent."* The truth of this seems apparent in the Yemen today.

Qat is credited with having its good qualities however, and like wine, has perhaps been created to make men glad. The tragedy is that it seems to be abused and that only the men are made happy, confirming again the frequent observation that the East is strictly a man's world.

PART VI

CHAPTER THIRTY

Bridging the Gap

ONE often felt that nothing, not even the war, could ever rouse Jidda from the stupor in which it seemed to live. The ways and customs of the past were so inbred, the sluggish momentum of living so unchanged from the far-gone Biblical days, that rumors of great developments to take place were accepted with the skeptical attitude that Islam seemed to engender. However, familiar with the present oilfield operations in the Al Hasa province on the Persian Gulf, as well as plans for rapid development of the desert's apparently inexhaustible oil resources, it was obvious to us that the outward flow of Arabia's black blood would result in a return flow of gold and that this sudden and increasing revenue would produce irresistible changes that none of the country's age-old barriers could in the end withstand.

Results of the increasing tempo of oil-field activities slowly reverberated throughout the land. Gold started to trickle into the king's treasury to incubate into astonishing rumors. The giant of Arabia began to stir, to look westward and grow conscious of the two thousand years during which it had slept.

The sudden fever of activity caused by our foreign oil expansion program had resulted by this time in capacity production of Arabian oil. In fact, the size of the Ras Tanura refinery had already been increased again from 50,000 barrels per day to 140,000. Now plans became known for further expansion and all possible exploitation of the proved reserves of approximately ten billion barrels of oil.* It was staggering to consider the difference between 15,000 barrels per day being produced prior to 1944 and the plans for production of 821,000 barrels per day by 1951. From our standpoint we, in Jidda, were not so much impressed by the value and need of this incomprehensible amount of oil to the United States and the world, as we were with the profound changes it would inevitably cause throughout Arabia.

The men responsible for these development plans acted with courage and foresight since at this time they might easily have assumed that with the end of the war and the curtailment of military demands, the world consumption of oil and oil products might conceivably return to a prewar level. We see now that with the war's end there was actually an amazing increase in American consumption, the United States Navy alone using such enormous quantities as could not be conveniently supplied by the United States and other areas combined.† This

---

* Of the world's estimated 100 billion barrels of *proved* oil reserves, a total of 48 billion are located here on Russia's doorstep—this virtually unprotected and politically volatile Middle Eastern area.

† It is interesting to note that the world consumption of oil is about 12 million barrels per day and that America alone uses more than half of this figure. Actually she uses about 7 million barrels per day, which is a million more than she produces.

fact of course was not foreseen during my Arabian days, nor was the fact that by 1951 the increasing world demands would provide an immediate outlet for such quantities of Arabian oil as could humanly be made available. It is only fortunate that these plans were formulated and followed to completion.

The oil company rapidly pushed the development of the Dhahran and Ras Tanura operations as well as their search for new fields. They started to lay a 12–14-inch pipe line from the new field at Abqaiq to Dhahran with talk of a second 14-inch line in the near future and a third 30–22–20-inch line from Abqaiq direct to the port of Ras Tanura. A second 12-inch line was begun from Dhahran to Ras Tanura and plans made for increasing the capacity of the line to Bahrein still more. They began the work of enlarging the capacities of the stabilizers and refineries at both Dhahran and Ras Tanura as the development of the Abqaiq field went steadily forward. Then in June (1945) the Qatif field was discovered, to be followed by the Ain Dar field, the Fadhili and the Ain Haradh fields. Each day brought new stories of plans for the development of the various fields discovered, but of more immediate interest to us were the unbelievable rumors of Saudi plans for spending the influx of gold.

The poverty of the Saudi government, having in the past been dependent principally on pilgrim fees for revenue, forced them to draw heavily upon advance royalties—royalties that had been cut during the curtailment of oil production at the beginning of the war. As the prospects for the future brightened, however, they continued not only to draw on future revenues but to consider how best they could spend the rising tide of gold which would in time follow.

By the end of 1950 this rising tide of gold was to reach the colossal figure of ninety million dollars, for at that time the oil company was to revise their 17-year-old agreement with the king and, from then on, instead of paying him the old royalty of thirty-four cents per barrel, were to make him an equal partner so that he might share on a fifty-fifty basis in all of Aramco's future profits. (The operating profit for 1951 is estimated to be $200 million, half of which goes to Abdul Aziz.)

The king was perhaps the only one who could fully grasp the significance of this turn in Arabian fortunes. It had always been his mission, after having united his nation, to raise its standard of living, to introduce improved methods, new skills, to provide education and medical care. While he had made extraordinary gains for an unproductive and impoverished country, the oil royalties at last provided him with the means of accomplishing life-long ambitions. He envisioned new roads, railroads, communications, schools, hospitals and improved port facilities, always aware of the mountains of opposition he would encounter. He had had a lifetime of experience in dealing with the fanaticism and backwardness inherent in the Bedouin character and creed and it would be of consuming interest to observe his progress.

At the king's request the oil company provided engineers and technical experts to advise him on the various projects he had in mind. The company had long since gained his confidence and worked with him in the closest co-operation, developing the oil resources under arrangements which would be of mutual advantage to Arabia as well as themselves. The developments were planned as a "partnership" in the general sense of the word and the king often refers to the company as his "partners" who are helping him in the economic development of his country.

On the king's side of the partnership it was planned that the oil developments should not only create greater Arab prosperity but that the royalties should build toward the country's economic independence represented by lasting improvements such as electrification of cities, paving of streets, construction of roads, better harbor facilities, the use of water resources where available for extension of agriculture, the building of airports and internal and international communication systems. To the Arab population it would mean opportunities to work, to learn trades and to improve their living conditions.

On the American side, while ultimate profits inspired Aramco's participation and co-operation, the direct and indirect advantages go far beyond that and cannot be overemphasized. It would require many pages to discuss them. One advantage is the supplying of needed oil to fuel and lubricate the machines of the Western world. Perhaps an even greater advantage to America, and the democratic world in general, lies in the opportunity for developing the lasting friendship and confidence of a people who occupy one of the most important strategic areas of the world. This area is not only the crossroads and bridge between East and West but probably the largest region outside the Western Hemisphere in which the agents and advocates of communism have secured no important foothold. With the use of private funds, and under private motivation, companies representing free enterprise in the Western world have been carrying forward programs of development in the Middle East that are paralleling the governmental action conceived under the Marshall Plan as a means of supporting free enterprise against the threat of communism. Like this governmental action, the programs of the oil companies help the countries in which they are engaged, but they also help the United States by raising bulwarks of defense against the spread of doctrines and ideologies which are opposed to our freedom, our prosperity, our way of life, peace and security.

One of the first major public projects to get under way was a railroad. On its own initiative Aramco had started to build a road inland from Dammam via Dhahran and Abqaiq. This was actually part of a plan conceived by the king for a railway from the Persian Gulf to his capital, Riyadh, a distance of about 370 miles. It was the first large project to be undertaken and involved the establishment of Dammam as a new, deep-water port by the construction of a seven-mile pier at which ocean-going freighters might discharge cargo. This was later made a strictly Saudi government project and has now been carried by them to completion, the rails ending in Riyadh.

Another immense project began to take active shape about this time which gave employment to many more thousands of Arabs. Since 1944 a proposal had been before the United States Government for the building of a pipe-line as a war measure and with government funds, from eastern Saudi Arabia to the Mediterranean. Aramco's parent companies completed their own engineering studies which confirmed that a pipe-line was both feasible and advantageous, and they decided to make the project a reality as a private undertaking between Aramco and an affiliated company which they formed, the Trans-Arabian Pipe Line Company.

The building of the line presented engineering problems never encountered before. The shipment of pipe and materials and the movement of men were larger in volume and involved longer overseas voyages than any previous single project outside a military undertaking. New ideas were introduced in fabricating the large 30-inch pipe; special equipment was built to handle and weld it mechanically and this in turn required the manufacture of mammoth-sized trucks and trailers capable of transporting railroad freight-carloads of fifty tons or more. Tires of new size and design were required for the trucks that hauled the 93-foot lengths of pipe across the soft sands to location.

Of equal importance and magnitude were the creation of supporting facilities that are usually provided by other agencies in the community life of more settled countries. The company had to build houses for their American personnel as well as quarters for the many Arab workers employed. This meant the creation of communities from the ground up; the furnishing and installation of water supplies, gas, electricity, telephones, sewage disposal, hospitals, schools, churches and mosques, laundries, restaurants and stores. They had to build, maintain and staff power plants, air-conditioning plants, commissaries, dining halls, garages, hardware stores, and machine and carpenter shops. The project necessitated the construction of roads and airfields, the operation of a private airline and of fifteen hundred cars and trucks.

With the completion of this tremendous undertaking many new records were to be established. It has proven to be the largest overseas construction project ever financed by private United States capital, costing 200 million dollars. It is now the largest crude-oil pipe-line in the world and covers a distance of nearly 1,100 miles, running from the Abqaiq and Qatif fields to Ras Tanura, then across the northern deserts to the Mediterranean port of Sidon in the Lebanon. The pipe-line delivers 350,000 barrels of oil each day to the storage tanks at Sidon which hold seven million barrels—more than all the oil pumped daily from all the United States wells. The line saves a fleet of 65 tankers by eliminating the ten-day, 3,600-mile trip around the Arabian Peninsula.

A fleet of ships carried three billion ton-miles of freight from America for the pipe-line project, including 265,000 tons of pipe alone. The job called for the construction of 930 miles of desert highway and the drilling of forty water wells that now supply water to 100,000 Bedouin and their flocks of half a million animals. Its completion means that Europe will now receive a much faster supply of oil from the Middle East and can cut down on its imports from the Western Hemisphere. Since the United States depends increasingly on imported oil, it also means that in addition to husbanding the reserves of the Western Hemisphere we can now supplement them with Arabian oil.

These activities in the setting of desert lands that previously had known only the soft tread of the camel and his Bedouin master, were of such enormous proportions as to make one think of some modern Aladdin and his magic lamp. Their effect was being felt throughout the length and breadth of the land. The various ministries in Jidda began to hum as the government studied plans for municipal water and electrical works for both Jidda and Mecca. A contract was awarded an American company to build a pipe-line from Jidda to a wadi one hundred miles distant where subterranean water was found in sufficient quantity to supply the city. Work began to improve our little airport to the size of an international airdrome with hard-surface runways capable of handling any size ship and any possible volume of traffic. The United States Army had already made such an airport at Dhahran with plans, after it had served our military purposes, of turning it over to the Saudi government for commercial operation.

Freighters began to arrive in Jidda loaded with all the equipment required for a nation-wide radio and telephone communications system. Work began on a new road to Mecca and one to Medina. It was even planned to fill in the ruts and holes of Jidda's lanes, replacing the soft carpet of dust with hard-surface paving. But only when an American company was authorized to tear down the ancient city wall did we realize that a modern transition was actually taking place. Plans for the removal of Jidda's crumbling mantle of protection seemed to symbolize a final weakening of Islam's opposition to Western civilization and the opening of Arabia to the modern advancements of the outside world.

CHAPTER THIRTY-ONE

The Sesame Mill

DONALD was growing up too. He was no longer a gangling fawn but had attained the handsomeness of full maturity. His dignified manners, poise and self-assurance indicated his realization of this fact. He had grown to the size of a *saluqi,* but in his own estimation was as large and powerful as the most noble stag that ever ruled a forest. His prancing gait and arched neck was that of an Arab stallion, and he carried his lyre-shaped horns as a banner of manhood. He was as vain as a peacock of such perfectly formed weapons and fully conscious of their beauty and potential destructiveness. In a reversion to juvenile pranks he was careful not to mar them nor to inflict a serious injury, only occasionally jabbing their sharp tips into one's leg in a reminding, playful sort of way.

A full-grown buck gazelle, if angered or injured, can be extremely dangerous, relying not so much on strength and agility as on his spear-like horns and razor-sharp hoofs. Anyone who did not know Donald was quite cautious of him. Sensing their fear only tickled his ego and flattered his vanity.

Maturity had not spoiled Donald's disposition, however. When hungry or lonesome he was as dependent as the frail young fawn he used to be. If ignored, he butted or rubbed against me for caressing and if denied the amount considered his due, pretended to be offended. He assumed an indignant air, stalked across the floor in an obvious pout and in reserved silence disdained, for only a little while, all overtures toward reconciliation.

Donald was not above an inquisitive investigation of the kitchen now, or even prancing into John's room on rounds of inspection. When young, and while Hamid was still with us, he had discreetly avoided these rooms as though they were death-traps and had rejected all friendly gestures of both Hamid and John; displaying unusual perception of human nature in recognizing the dangerous purpose of their friendliness. He had observed Hamid with contempt as the old man subtly fingered his carving knife, a hungry glint in his eye, while offering friendship in a titbit. Any offered morsel was beneath Donald's interest but John was more successful, or at least tolerated. He served Donald's tea each afternoon before anyone else, heavily sweetened, steaming hot and accompanied by lavish portions of whatever sweetmeats appeared. John beamed with pleasure when Donald could not resist the temptation and fairly drooled as he felt of Donald's thigh, fancying the juicy haunch browning in a roasting pan.

Yes, Donald was aware of their crafty, ulterior thoughts and viewed their every gesture with justified suspicion; but he was grown now, master of Beit Najib and afraid of no one. However, he could still seem ridiculous to me. All dignity vanished as an affectation whenever he slipped on the tiling or whenever he had difficulty in reaching an inconsequential decision.

With the fullness of virile manhood, Donald became increasingly restless. He pranced about like a show-horse and spent hours gazing dreamily desertward through the open window. I presumed that it was the "call of the wild," "spring in his blood" or simply an overindulgence in tea. He stood immobile at the window, but for the flick of his ridiculous tail, a far-away look in his limpid brown eyes. Suddenly his ears were cast forward as if expecting to see something of interest in the distant brown hills. His glistening coat of reddish brown faded on the sides to silver and was neatly set off by a snow-white seat and belly-vest. He was as immaculate as any waiting bridegroom.

The gazelle's maturity and the question of exercise was an increasing problem. Only on the desert was he free to run as he liked, yet I became fearful of losing him there. I decided one afternoon to take him for a walk through the city instead, for Fred had told me of a sesame mill which sounded of interest. Zaid claimed he knew where the mill was located and agreed to accompany me there since it was easy to get lost among the dusty network of passages that veined the crumbling city.

I followed Zaid as he trod barefoot through the narrow alleys, his white-gowned figure turning first one way and then another until coming to the *suq*. Our appearance in the market place brought all activity to a near standstill. People stood in their tracks to stare at the gazelle trotting at my heels, enabling us to weave a way through the crowd without difficulty. We never turned to see if Donald followed, for I knew that although he would stop to smell or investigate, he would not let us precede him very far.

Emerging from the covered bazaars, Zaid followed a crooked lane just wide enough for us to brush past the few Arabs or donkeys encountered along the way. The light gray dust enveloped our feet with each step, cushioning the sound as would a deep-pile carpet. The jutting balconies almost met in places overhead, permitting little light to reach the shadowed lanes. Eventually we came upon an open courtyard of hard-packed ground interposed between several gray buildings with a shoulder-high wall on the alley side.

A crude mill had been erected in the courtyard. It was contrived by placing a tremendous round millstone flat upon a base of coral blocks. Another similar millstone was placed on the first and it turned on an axle that arose perpendicular from the center of the lower stone. A heavy pole had been fixed into a hole in the rim of the upper stone and extended horizontally perhaps ten feet outward. By pushing or pulling this pole the top stone could be made to revolve, and this job fell to a large but very aged camel.

Two heavy leather straps ran from the camel's collar to a singletree that was attached to the pole. By throwing his weight into the collar, the camel could move the stone, and uncounted years of his labor had taught him just how much effort was required to move it at a given, steady rate. He had worn a trench round the mill in a perfect circle. The inside strap received more slack than the outside one, so his side nearest the mill was fairly unscarred. His other side, however, received the constant rubbing and had become worn into one long streak of callosity. It had suffered and healed many times until becoming excrescent. It was hugely scabbed, coarser than rhinoceros hide, yet, despite the years of friction, became in places, long areas of pustuled flesh that could hardly be called flesh but rather malignant matter. Swarms of black flies fed upon him.

As the camel walked, slowly pulling the pole, the strap sawed with each step into one long red gash from which dark blood slowly trickled down his coarse, wrinkled hide. He wore no blinkers to keep him on his steady round from sunup to sundown. This was unnecessary. Another precaution had been taken so that he would forever go on his given round by instinct and memory and the feel of his harness; never wavering by one step, but plodding on without change or variation. To insure such action, he had been blinded.

It reminded me of a similar scene in Isfahan where I had found blinded camels grinding poppy seed in opium mills secreted in dark cellars.

The sesame seed was poured into slots toward the center of the upper wheel and in its turning they slipped down to be crushed and to gradually work outward, along with their oil, into a trough running around the stone. This mash would be scooped up and placed in a crude press to extract the oil used for cooking.

A similar but smaller mill was operated by a little donkey. He had not been blinded but wore blinkers. His side was as deeply cut, scarred and calloused and his work just as miserable—for he was crippled. He had one club foot. He hobbled pitifully on three legs, not touching the ground with his deformity but straining in his yoke, round and round, steadily and without change, every hobble cutting my heart as the strap did his damaged, cicatrixed side.

The miller was just a plain, average man. He did not look more cruel or insensitive than any other Arab. I knew it would be useless to remonstrate with him; so to Zaid, who avoided my eyes, I gave several riyals to go and purchase *berseem*. When he returned I caught the surprised donkey by his halter. Thrusting an armful of clover into his unbelieving face, I silently promised to choke his owner if he objected. He did not object but stared stupidly, wondering why we should be so kind to a dumb animal. Zaid halted the plodding camel and fed him also. The once noble, independent beast mouthed the green suc-

culence placidly, without any show of gratitude. The small donkey
seemed much more grateful. I determined to buy him. He was worth
very little, and several Egyptian pounds could replace him. I knew
it would be easy to persuade Aziz to let him graze free and unworked
among his own flocks.

Taking three pounds from my pocket, I offered them to the Arab,
explaining that with these he could buy a younger and stronger donkey.
His greedy eyes shifted from the money to the crippled donkey, then
to Donald and back to the money again. Zaid only stared, unable to
understand.

Adding several riyals to the pounds, I declared that I'd give no more.
As the miller hesitated, weighing the proposition, I started to return
the money to my pocket, but he grabbed my arm saying that I could
have the donkey in return for the gazelle.

"Donald?" I asked in shocked surprise. I felt ready to upbraid him
for such an insolent suggestion, but suddenly an idea entered my head.
After enough bargaining to satisfy the custom, and with a show of
uncertainty, I finally consented with his assurance that he would be
kind to the gazelle. Zaid, however, could control himself no longer.
His mouth hung open and he rolled his eyes.

"La, la! Mister Bob," he protested, as if we were selling a son. "He
eat Donald!" cried the boy as if I didn't know it.

"*Maleesh*, Zaid. *Maleesh*," I said in a placating voice, slyly passing
a wink which silenced him.

Turning to the miller, I repeated my acceptance of the trade, providing he would not tie the gazelle up but would let him have the
freedom of the compound. This he was willing to do, since he probably
intended to butcher him as soon as our backs were turned. After
forcing him to absolve me from any further responsibility once we
had passed through the gate, I bid Zaid lead out the little donkey.

He unfastened the animal reluctantly and throwing a rope around his neck, led him out, his perplexed gaze fastened upon me.

Handing the money to the miller as *baksheesh,* I patted Donald's head in a promissory manner and slipped out the gate. "Come on, Zaid," I said encouragingly. Feeling ready to burst, I added, "Never mind, Zaid. Just wait."

We headed down the narrow lane, Zaid scuffing his black feet in the dust with the little donkey hobbling behind. When we passed beyond the mill-compound, I stopped long enough to make one long, sharp whistle. A brown-and-silver streak bounded over the compound wall and trotted up to join us.

Zaid giggled foolishly all the way home.

CHAPTER THIRTY-TWO

That Compelling Instinct

WE RESISTED the advance of prickly heat, that invention of hell, by every means known to medical science, but since the body could never be kept dry, it never healed. The itching pain of the rash was maddening as it crept insidiously over the entire skin, creating a raw mass of eruption in its progress.

As if this was not enough to shake one's courage, I developed a kidney stone. It was probably caused by the condensed seawater and by constant perspiration. Although one might consume gallons of liquids they were all lost in perpetual sweat, permitting certain minerals to settle and form sharp crystals—a common complaint in Arabia. The one doctor in Jidda to whom I had access, was a withered little Indian who operated a small dispensary maintained by the Indian

Legation. The poor man was only equipped with a stethoscope and a few bottles of medicine, but he did give me a few grains of morphine and advised me to eat plenty of watermelon! I felt too abused by the climate to ask where he thought I might obtain them. However, in the intensity of a spasm, the morphine at least afforded a little relief to the dagger in my side.

The penetrating damp heat added to the discomfort and I longed to throw open the back shutters in a gesture of defiance to both climate and custom. But the shutters had to remain closed, otherwise I would have viewed the latticed windows of Arab harems, as if that could be a sop to my torture. We were tolerated infidels and had to be careful not to offend in any way.

A severe attack one afternoon left me trembling in a bed wet with sweat and smeared from grating sores. Donald stood beside the bed regarding me with a detached camel-look. He stretched closer as I became aware of him and began to lick my hand as though something had penetrated his inadequate brain. I drew him to me in a weak moment of self-pity and dampened his silken neck. "Poor Donald," I cried. "You foolish creature. You don't know what it is to be sick and lonely in a foreign land!"

Donald thoughtfully rubbed his sensitive horns slowly back and forth under my fondling hand and, discerning my unwillingness to play, again stretched forward for a puzzled examination, comforting in his primitive solicitude but tickling me into laughter. The tragi-comic aspects of the scene emerged and I pushed him away.

"Enough of this!" I said. "Where's Sayed?" to which he pricked up his ears. "We'll have a drink, and we'll go to Cairo too," I promised. "We've been here too long, but we won't stay to die in this neglected place and be buried in that Potter's field reserved for Christian dogs. We'll have a drink and forget this damned climate!"

Stroking the gazelle's velvet nose consoled me more than it did him. With true Arab philosophy he thought the situation quite all right. When Sayed appeared in answer to my call, I told him, "Sayed, *gib shwiya moiya, shwiya lemon, kebir Melotti,*" ("Little water, little lemon but lots of gin.") "I have such a pain, I think I die zigzag!"

Sayed was not disturbed. *"Tyeeb, tyeeb,"* he muttered and, anxious to please, trotted off to do my bidding. When he delivered the refreshment, Donald tried to climb upon my shoulder in an effort to reach the glass I held. Feeling too weak to argue, I said,

"Well, what the devil," while lowering the glass. "Why not. Dickie and John slip you a drink when I'm not looking and for all I know you may need it as badly as I do!"

We were both in bed and off to a good start toward forgetting our troubles when Fred appeared. "Are you still alive?" he asked in a tone which implied that any condition would be all the same to him.

"Yes," I said with a sigh, "but if I survive, which I seriously doubt, I'll be able to say the same as Arthur!"

Only Allah knew what the forty years in Jidda had accomplished with the poor old carcass of Arthur's. Yet he always depreciated the hard life he had led, only adding in his inimitable whisper, "No, it's not been too bad. I can get about and attend to my business. I'm still as fit as any man. Of course I've lost my memory . . ."

Fred laughed, probably thinking of Arthur's justification. "No," he said. *"You* haven't been here forty years yet!"

My "affliction" had improved to the point where it seemed I might survive, when Pat lured me out of the house for a ride on the desert. He drove slowly through the alleyways, heading for the Mecca Gate. The few people abroad made way for our jeep to stop and stare in admiration at the handsome gazelle standing on the back seat. Once through the gate, we took the rolling Mecca road and sped past loaded camels and trudging Arabs. Near the foothills we turned onto a hard level spot of desert where the gazelle could run off his energy. Before coming to a halt, however, he leaped from the jeep and bounded away as if stung by a bee. We too felt suddenly wild and free and so grateful for the descending coolness that we walked the desert until the red sun settled into the sea.

When the mauve-colored hills faded into solid, deep shadow we called for the gazelle so that we might return home. He readily returned but would not get in the jeep nor would he let us touch him; so we decided to let him pace the jeep until tired enough to get in. The mischievous animal followed indifferently as we slowly headed toward town. Whenever we stopped we found him still to be in a tantalizing mood and although I coaxed and threatened, he kept his distance. I even offered a cigarette, which he snatched before jumping beyond reach.

We were obliged to proceed slowly, becoming more and more exasperated, for it was already quite dark. Donald followed at a slow trot until a string of busses suddenly rattled past, headed for Mecca. They must have frightened or confused him by their noise and glare, for he turned and chased after them. We quickly turned around and sped back but he had disappeared. He could be found nowhere although we stopped every little distance to call and whistle.

Pat and I spent several hours searching up and down the quiet desert without success. To my weary appeal for advice what next to do, Pat said that he "hadn't a clue." In the end we decided to go home and look again in the morning. Donald had been lost several times before and had always been brought home for the reward, so I was not overly anxious.

Next day we were all out early covering the desert in every direction, not so fearful of the dogs catching the gazelle, since he could outrun them, but of the Bedouin or pilgrims whom he might approach for food. I posted large rewards and news of the loss quickly spread about town. Nevertheless, we spent days in fruitless effort, always hopeful that if not we, someone else might be successful and bring him home. Even John joined in the effort. He at first felt cruelly frustrated, considering the possibility of someone else feasting upon something he had so patiently fattened, but then John awoke to realize that he too held a tender affection for the animal. Undecided how to handle such an unusual emotion, he declared with affected heartlessness, "Oh, some pilgrim will probably find Donald. He'll think it's a gift from Allah to be sacrificed at Muna!" John's booming voice, however, was but a spurious sound.

It was not talked about, but melancholia inhabited Beit Najib. The dispirited servants announced several times each day that a Bedou at the door insisted the forlorn creature at the end of a rope was our pet. They refused to leave until I announced in person, "No, no. Thank you, but that's not my gazelle," and while the dark faces around me retained their funereal expressions, I endeavored to explain that Donald could not be mistaken; he was sleek and handsome and wore a collar about his neck.

I continued to search whenever the time could be spared and questioned more Bedou on the desert about town than I knew existed there. When I inquired if they had seen a gazelle they looked at me as though I were feeble-minded and assured me, yes, of course they had seen a gazelle!

"Fain? Fain?" I eagerly asked. They always retained a bewildered look and only waved vaguely toward the hills.

"But have you seen *my* gazelle?" I impatiently added, mopping the sweat from my face. They seemed maddeningly incapable of understanding that it had to be a certain gazelle and thought me mentally deranged when I insisted that not just any gazelle would do. These unsuccessful encounters always terminated by my dashing somewhat frantically on while both the Bedou and I muttered quite different things to ouselves. I began to feel a deep sympathy for the distraught Hagar.

While resting beneath a samr tree I heard no murmurings, however, except those of my own imagination, seeing Donald wandering about, lonesome and hungry and unable to care for himself. I tried to console myself by thinking that if only he had eluded the dogs, perhaps he was better off. I had been in Arabia a long time and would soon be leaving. It would never be possible to take him with me, or if I found a way, Donald would only die in a colder climate. He had been a companion in my isolation and had made my life more bearable. That should be enough, but, nevertheless, I continued on.

My searches along the parched coastal plain finally led me as far as the ruined foothills. I slowly realized that I had not loved merely a friendless, dependent creature, a gentle little animal. He represented much more than that. It appeared painfully true that all things in life are as transient as the very warmth and shadows created by the rising or setting sun. They appear, perform some function and then vanish; leaving either a refreshed spot or a sad ache in the heart.

On the tenth day of the gazelle's absence I was bumping across the sand dunes far to the north when I jumped a pair of gazelles. They bounded off at high speed for a short space when the buck suddenly stopped and turned to regard me.

I screeched quickly to a standstill and leaped out. "Donald!" I shouted, for it was he. The little collar and name tag were still about his neck. The tag was a silver Saudi riyal on which I had chiseled: DONALD, AMERICAN LEGATION, JIDDA, SAUDI ARABIA.

Donald stood proudly erect with ears eagerly forward. He stamped a foot, snorted and playfully tossed his head before turning to look after the waiting doe and back to me again—still unable to make a quick decision. I approached closer, pleading softly to him. Suddenly he trotted forward to my outstretched hand, to smell me gladly and to let me put my arms about him.

Fondling him, I glanced across the great sweep of the lonely Rakba plain which we knew so well together, and on to the placid sea beyond. It was burnished to a reddened bronze by the evening glory of the Red Sea sun. My lips felt the velvet of Donald's soft muzzle as I ran a hand down his neck to unfasten the buckle that denied his freedom.

When I arose from the sand Donald looked behind him, then hesitantly, as if waiting to be recalled, he turned and trotted toward the anxious doe. I saw her reach out to touch him. Then with the flick of two small black tails, they both started without a backward glance, in easy graceful lopes toward their own native habitat, the distant evening purple of the low Hijaz hills.

CHAPTER THIRTY-THREE

The Broken Mantle

MANY things were happening in Arabia with confusing suddenness. Our mission was drawing to a close, its work accomplished. The British members had received their orders to return to Egypt and Pat, Dickie and John left, leaving only Fred and me to wind up the final threads of our joint adventure. The legation would take over where we left off, but the particular program that we represented had been fulfilled and it was felt by our respective governments that Arabia no longer needed this extra assistance.

The critical situation that existed in Saudi Arabia at the beginning of the war had been relieved by our mutual Anglo-American aid. The lending of financial assistance and the supplying of all the most essential commodities necessary to overcome the country's economic distress had by now eased the strains imposed by war. But more important, this assistance had firmly secured a substantial contribution toward winning the struggle. Arabia had been unable to render any military service but our help had enabled Abdul Aziz to maintain stability in the Arab world at a time when instability or uncontrolled pro-Axis sympathies could easily have placed this highly strategic region in the hands of the enemy.

Back in 1941 the British Army had experienced a narrow escape in the German-inspired revolt in Iraq. Their Ninth and Tenth Armies in Palestine, Syria and Iraq had been reduced to a skeleton force during the time when their Ninth Army was being hard pressed by Rommel in the North African campaign. To have had the Arab tribes on a rampage in the British rear, or in conspiracy with the Germans, would have been fatal. Although there were many Axis sympathizers among the Arabs, Abdul Aziz remained staunchly on the side of the Allies and had tolerated no disloyalty wherever his influence extended. In the absence of his steadying hand, the Allies would have had to maintain order in Arabia by the use of occupying forces and this would have cost far more than did the aid which we had given. Our purpose was accomplished and at a meager price.*

---

* Saudi Arabia's contribution to the war effort is described in the citation of the Legion of Merit, Degree of Chief Commander, presented in 1947 to King Ibn Saud by President Truman. The citation reads in part: "His Majesty Abdul Aziz Ibn Abdur Rahman Al Faisal Al Saud, King of Saudi Arabia, rendered exceptionally meritorious service to the war effort of the United Nations. He led his country in an unwavering course of support and encouragement to the cause of the Allies. . . . As Commander-in-Chief of Saudi Arabia he kept the land, sea and air routes under his control open for use, and by his attitude of wholehearted cooperation, he enabled American forces to accomplish a program of construction and resource development in the country that derived benefits of major proportions for the prosecution of the war. Through his unswerving loyalty, and his dynamic leadership at the head of his nation in the support of the cause, King Abdul Aziz Ibn Saud made a notable contribution to the successful war effort of the United Nations."

Now the war was won and Arabia's oil resources were providing the means toward the country's economic independence. This was evident wherever we turned. Crews of American engineers and boatloads of machinery began to arrive in Jidda for the work of supplying municipal water and electricity; for the construction of roads, the paving of streets, the building of airports, the improvement of Jidda's quays and the building of a Saudi radio station. On the Red Sea, as on the Persian Gulf, thousands of Arabs who had never dreamed of any work beyond tending flocks, were learning how to work in machine shops, run power machines, work at lathes, drive complex trucks, hoists and bulldozers. In company training schools they were learning many technical skills; the operation of communication equipment, airplanes, railroads, refineries, power and air-conditioning plants. It was the beginning of a new era in Arabian history, and oil was responsible for it all.

The Middle East had been proven to contain the greatest oil reserves of any one region in the world, the reserves available in fields already discovered nearly equaling the proved reserves remaining in the known fields of the entire Western Hemisphere. This oil is of vital importance to our own continued prosperity and security, as well as that of the whole democratic world; and in it too, lies the opportunity for an Arab renaissance which, if unhampered by the catastrophe of another war, might match, if not far surpass, the illustrious accomplishments of their past.

The second great war of modern times had just been won, but already the clouds of another were gathering on our immediate horizon, threatening to destroy the vital treasures of the Middle East and the free nations which they supported. The enemy was but a short march or a few hours flight away, his proximity felt and his intentions known, and yet these treasures were not protected, nor could they be properly defended against his attack from the place where they existed.

We felt ready to go home. The feeling of satisfaction in a worthy cause accomplished was marred by doubts of its endurance. Yet the throbbing force of an awakened nation brought hope and there was gratification in seeing the great transition begin that would bridge the gap of two thousand years time, and in knowing that we had had some part in its birth.

It was with some regret that we prepared to leave Arabia, although we were no longer a small and privileged group of pioneers. A certain fraternal spirit had vanished and we began to feel strange in a little town that we had grown to understand and to care for in just the way it had always been. Something departed along with our friends and with the destruction of the old city wall, but just as surely did a fresh and invigorating spirit appear. No longer did a hushed and furtive atmosphere inhabit the town, making it seem as lifeless as an ancient city of the dead. The cleansing sea breeze and desert air now entered, driving out the breath of multitudes long past, and leaving a sense of vitality which Jidda and Arabia had never known.

Glossary

ABAYA—(or aba) a long, close-fitting cloak, usually black, with a bit of embroidery at collar, sleeves and cuffs

AGAL—(or iqal) headropes or woolen cord wrapped double around the head and holding the headcloth in place

AIWA—yes

AKHNATON—Egyptian pharaoh (1375–1357 B.C.) XVIII dynasty, who held that the solar monotheism was absolute

AL—of the family of, the

AL HAMDU L'ILLAH—praise be to God

AL KHARJ—an oasis in the Najd south of Riyadh

ALLAHU AKBAR—(or Allah al-Akbar) God is omnipotent

ALLAH YIBARAK FIK—God bless you

ALLAH YI'RIF—only God knows

AL'UMRA—the little pilgrimage

ANA MESKEEN—I am poor

AQABA—the name of a spot outside Mecca where stand three pillars which are called the three devils

ARAFAT—a mount near Mecca on the plain of Arafat, better called Jabal al Rahma, the Mount of Mercy

BAKSHEESH—a gift, alms

BAYAD—a fish of the Red Sea

BEDAWI—a plural form of Bedou or Bedouin

BEDIE—heavy cloak of the Bedouin, made of goat wool

BEDOU—the same as Bedouin. For either singular or plural

BEDOUIN—wanderers or nomads, desert dwellers. Can be used in this form for either singular or plural

BEIT—house

BEIT ALLAH—house of God, the Kaaba in Mecca

BERSEEM—a clover-like plant raised for animal food

BINT—girl

BISMI'ALLAH—in the name of God

BRAZIER—a vessel holding hot coals

BURQA—part of the Kiswa, the silk and cotton covering for the Kaaba

CHIT—a note

CIRCUMAMBULATION—in the pilgrimage to Mecca, the rite of circling the Kaaba, commonly called "Tawaf," or "Tawif"

DAHANA—an 800 mile narrow belt of sand of deep orange color in eastern Arabia, running between the Great Nefudh in the north and Rub' Al Khali in the south. One of the most distinctive geographic features of Saudi Arabia

DAR—towered houses of the Yemen

DHOB—a desert lizard

DHOBI—laundry boy

DHOW—Arab boat of the Red Sea

DHUL-HIJJA—month of the pilgrimage, the 12th month in the Arab calendar

DHURRA—corn

DRAGOMAN—Egyptian guide

DUKHN—millet

EFFENDI—clerk or interpreter, a title equivalent to "mister" and usually assumed by white collar workers

EL IHRAM—the prescribed dress for the Hajj consisting of two lengths of toweling, and meaning "mortification"

EMIR—(or Amir) an Arabian military commander, chieftain or ruler. Also a title given to descendants of Mohammed through his daughter Fatima

ENTA—you, you are

FAIN—where

FELLAHEEN—Egyptian field laborers

FILOOS—money

FUTA—a sarong or skirt, in Yemen, usually worn ankle length

GAHWA—coffee

GALABIYA—a plain gown worn by servants or the laboring class in Arab countries

GAMOOSE—water buffalo

GHEE—clarified butter made from goat or camel milk

GIRSH—small Arabian coin

GREAT NEFUDH—an area of about 22,000 square miles of rolling reddish sand in the northern part of Saudi Arabia

HAJAR EL ASWAD—the sacred Black Stone of the Kaaba

HAJJ—the pilgrimage to Mecca

HAJJI—one who has attended the Arafat ceremony while on the pilgrimage. All pilgrims are called Hajjis however, for it is assumed they will perform all necessary ceremonies entitling them to this title.

HAJJIANS—camel cavalry or mounted soldiers of the Najd

HAMMAM—bathroom or lavatory

HEIVA 'ALA-SSALAH—come to prayer. The call of the Muezzin

HIJAZ—(or Hejaz) the province of Saudi Arabia bordering on the Red Sea

HIJRAH—flight. It refers to Mohammed's flight from Mecca to Medina in 622 A.C. and is used as the basis for calculating the Moslem era. Before and after the "Hijrah."

HOORIE—a small Arab boat carved from the trunk of a tree

HOWDAH—An Indian word for a canopied frame which is strapped to the backs of camels for carrying passengers. Also called a palanquin. The Arabic word is shagdoof.

HUBBUK—water-pipe

HUJRAH—place of Mohammed's tomb in Medina

IBN—son of

ID AL ADHA—the Festival of the Sacrifice

IHRAN—cotton headcloth, same as qhotra

IJMA—a supplement to the Koran, being a collection of principles as expressed by the Prophet Mohammed

IKHWAN—Arabian society, Ikhwan al Muslimeen, "brotherhood of Muslims." They are settlers and bear arms in times of national emergency.

IMAM—king. Also meaning the spiritual and temporal head of Islam. A leader of prayers. Any of the 12 heads of Islam recognized by the Shiites.

INSHA' ALLAH—if God wills, or, God willing

ISLAM—meaning "submission" (to the Will of God). The religion of Moslems

ISMA—listen, or, hey you!

JABAL AL RAHMA—the Mount of Mercy, a spot near Mecca

JIHAD—a Moslem holy war

KAABA—the holy temple in Mecca

KEBIR—(or kabir) large

KHAMSIN—hot southwest wind, a wind-storm

KISWA—(or Kesoua) silk and cotton embroidered covering for the Kaaba. Also known as the Mahmal

KITIR—many or much

KORAN—the sacred book of the Moslems as divinely revealed to the founder of Islam, the Prophet Mohammed

KUFI—(or kofya) a skull cap worn under the headcloth, the plural being kufia or kufias

KWAYIS—good

LA—no

LABAN—curdled camel milk

LA ILAHA ILLAAL-LAH! MOHAMMEDUN RASULUAL-LAH—the profession of faith of the Moslem religion which means "there is no god but Allah, Mohammed is His Messenger!" The flag of Saudi Arabia carries this creed.

MABRAJ—(or mabraz) a room in Yemen used for relaxation

MAFEESH—there is none, or it is finished

MAHMAL—the Kaaba covering, newly made each year and customarily presented to the Keeper of the Keys of the Kaaba and accompanied by many gifts for the poor.

MAKANIKI—mechanic

MAKTOUB—it is written

MALEESH—nevermind, or, it doesn't matter

MAYA KADENSA—water condenser

MESHRABIYA—a wooden screen or intricate lattice work

MESJID EL HARAM—the Great Mosque in Mecca which surrounds the Kaaba

MISHLAH—the outer Arab robe of fine camel wool

MOSLEM—one who believes in the faith established by the Prophet Mohammed

MUEDDIN—same as muezzin

MUEZZIN—Moslem crier of the hour for prayer

MUHASSIR—a wadi between Arafat and Muzdalifa

MULLAH—a learned teacher or expounder of the religion of Islam

MULTAZAM—the wall of the Kaaba holding the Black Stone

MUTAWAS—teachers or instructors of Islam

MUTAWWIFS—licensed guides in the holy land of Islam

MUZDALIFA—the name of a spot on the plain near Mecca

NAJD—(or Nejd) a province of Saudi Arabia toward the Persian Gulf

NEFUDH—see Great Nefudh

NOM—(or na'am) interrogative, "what," otherwise "yes"

ORYX—a large, white, straight-horned antelope

PASHA—an Egyptian title conferred only by the king of Egypt—not hereditary

PARIAH—an outcast, one rejected by society. Wild dogs.

PURDAH—the custom of going veiled, seclusion in the harem

QAT—a Yemeni shrub

QHOTRA—(or gotra) a cotton or woolen kerchief used for a headcloth

HARAKHTI—the sun or the name applied to the sun by the ancient Egyptians who considered it the supreme god.

—part of the coastal plain bordering the Red Sea

—(or Ramadhan) the 9th month of the year. The month of . The month in which the Koran was first revealed.

rabian silver coin, worth about thirty cents U.S.

—a raised, built-in wall seat

B' AL KHALI—the "Empty Quarter" an area in southern Arabia covering 250,000 square miles of desert sand, making it the largest continuous body of sand in the world.

SABAH AL-HEIR—may your morning be bright

SABAH AN-NOUR—may your morning be bright also

SAFA AND MARWA—the two hills outside Mecca involved in the ceremony of Sa'i

SAFRAGI—a servant who performs the duties of a butler

SA'I—the ceremony of running between the points of Safa and Marwa

SALAAM—a gesture of greeting made by bowing the head while touching the forehead and then the heart

SALAAM ALAIKUM—peace be on you

SALUKI—a breed of dog used for hunting gazelles, its history going back into antiquity

SAMBOOK—a small Arab sailing boat

SAMBUSA—fried dough containing meat

SAMEK—fish

SHAMIYAH—wooden screen or intricately carved lattice work, the same as meshrabiya

SHEIKH—literally, old man. An Arab chief. Also a title of respect

SHI—tea

SHIITE—one of that branch of the Moslem faith who rejects the first three caliphs and considers Ali, Mohammed's son-in-law, as the first rightful successor of Mohammed, and who do not acknowledge the Sunna as any part of the Law.

SHUFTI—look

SHUMAL—a north wind, usually containing heavy rain

SIMOOM—hot desert wind-storm

SOMALI—a native of Somaliland

SUNNA—the theory and practice of orthodox Islam.

SUNNITE—one of a Moslem sect who acknowledge the first three caliphs to be the rightful successors of Mohammed

SUQ—bazaar or market place

SURA—a chapter from the Koran

TAKRUNI—(pl. Takarina) people made up of various black t̶ Africa

TALBIYA—a recital made by the pilgrim

TARBUSH—a fez or Moslem hat, worn mostly in Egypt and Tu̶

TARIK—road or trail

TAWIF—the ritual of circuiting the Kaaba, circumambulation

THOB—long white undergarment worn under the mishlah

TAWIF EL WIDAA—the circuit (of the Kaaba) of farewell

TIHAMA PLAIN—the coastal plain of Arabia bordering the Red Sea

TYEEB—good

ULEMA—body of church elders learned in Moslem theology and law

WA-ALAIKUM ES-SALAAM—and on you peace

WADI—a dry river bed in the strict sense, which is dry in Arabia throughout much of the year. Long shallow depressions are also given this name.

WAHHABI—a Moslem sect, a branch of the Sunnites

WALAD—boy

YAUM AL TARWIYA—the exodus from Mecca to Muna

ZAKAAT—(charity) the second great pillar on which the structure of Islam stands. In their order, these four pillars are prayer, charity, fasting and pilgrimage.

ZIYARAT—the pilgrimage to Medina